BRADY BRADY BRADY

BRADY BRADY BRADY

The Complete Story of THE BRADY BUNCH as Told by the Father/Son Team Who Really Know

Sherwood Schwartz • Lloyd J. Schwartz

Creator and Executive Producer of *The Brady Bunch*

Producer of *The Brady Bunch*

Foreword by Monty Hall

RUNNING PRESS
PHILADELPHIA • LONDON

9 8 7 6 5 4 3 2 1
Digit on the right indicates the number of this printing

Library of Congress Control Number: 2010922442

ISBN 978-0-7624-3962-1

Cover and interior design by Corinda Cook
Edited by Greg Jones
Typography: Garamond, Helvetica Neue, and Typography of Coop

All photographs courtesy of Lloyd Schwartz.

Running Press Book Publishers
2300 Chestnut Street
Philadelphia, PA 19103-4371

Visit us on the web!
www.runningpress.com

I dedicate this book to my wife, Mildred.
For me, it was love at first sight,
and so far it has lasted sixty-eight years.

—Sherwood Schwartz

To my father.
Read what I've written. You'll see why.

—Lloyd Schwartz

Contents

Foreword

It takes a special art to balance the emotional elevator ups and downs of a single family, but a blended family of two different mindsets, DNA, and provoking lifestyles is indeed a creative challenge.

Not for Sherwood Schwartz and his son Lloyd, who "blended" their talents together to write *Brady, Brady, Brady*—an intimate, behind-the-scenes look at one of the most successful family series in TV history, *The Brady Bunch*.

It was a statistic in 1965—which said that 30 percent of all marriages involve offspring from a previous marriage—that caught Sherwood's inquiring mind, giving bloom to 117 episodes, three specials, and two feature films.

Culling from Sherwood's long and loving marriage and the success of his children, life experiences can be transferred to any family. This book is a tribute to both father and son (with a bit of insight from mother, Mildred Schwartz, thrown in no doubt). I've always thought Mildred was as funny as Sherwood in that forest of humor.

—Monty Hall

Preface

A word about *Brady, Brady, Brady*.

This is an unusual book. Many books have been written by two authors together, but the two parts of this book were written by two authors independently.

Sherwood Schwartz wrote the first section about the creation of *The Brady Bunch* series, and his partner and son, Lloyd J. Schwartz, wrote the second and third parts about the production of the show and its legacy.

They didn't collaborate in the traditional sense, because they wanted readers to appreciate their individual perspectives. So, if they write about some of the same things, they hope their views of the events will be somewhat different and enlightening.

It was certainly enlightening to them.

Acknowledgements

This book would never have been finished without the help of my personal assistant, Bonnie Kalisher Dukes. Thanks to Mrs. Dukes for her patience in keeping track of the many rewrites—only God and Bonnie know how many of those there have been—plus all the articles, photos, clippings, graphs, and drawings from 1967 to the present.

Very special thanks to my son, Lloyd, who went from dialogue coach for the Brady kids, to associate producer, and finally producer in the space of six years. It took me 25 years to make those moves.

And special thanks to his encyclopedic mind for detail, not only for all the episodes, but also for the various permutations and combinations of "Brady" projects from the two-hour specials to the spin-offs and features; and if I've left anything out, for all else as well, because my own memory is no longer as good as it never was. Thanks also, in alphabetical order, to all my co-workers, friends, and other helpmates regarding specific events and conversations, some as long as 41 years ago: ABC, Jack Arnold, Jim Aubrey, Jim Backus, Blanche Baker, Cecil Barker, Bob Blumofe, Joyce Bulifant, Captain Pettito, CBS, Hank Coleman, Steve Cox, Doug Cramer, Ann B. Davis, Frank De Vol, Bob Denver, Barry Diller, Mike Eisner, F.C.C., Fluffy, Dabs Greer, Monty Hall, Florence Henderson, Howard Anderson Company, Jeff Hunter, Ed James, Lauren Johnson, Paul King, Christopher Knight, Jimmy Komack, Bruce Lansbury, Emmett Lavery, Mike Lookinland, Monte Margetts, Maureen McCormick, Hattie McDaniel, NBC, Susan Olsen, William S. Paley, Paramount, Eve Plumb, Robert Reed, John Reynolds, John Rich, Irv Robbins, Peter Robinson, Floyd Schwartz, Lloyd Schwartz, Mildred Schwartz, Solomon & Finger Co., Hunt Stromberg Jr., Tiger, Frances Whitfield, Barry Williams, Writers Guild, and George Wyle.

And especially to my wife, Mildred, who came up with the book title *Brady, Brady, Brady*.

—Sherwood Schwartz

Read my father's acknowledgements and add my acknowledgements to those acknowledgments. Just skip the part about me.

In addition I'd like to acknowledge my wife, Barbara; my sons, Andy and Elliot; and Andy's wife, Lindsay; as well as many people who have listened to me telling these stories for far too many years. Indeed, they have had to endure a lot of reliving the past while putting up with me in the present.

Some people who have helped me along the Brady way: Peter Baldwin, Larry Becsey, Ralph Berge, Bruce Bilson, Mike Blue, Marshall Coben, Adam Conger, Roger Cruz, John Cygan, Paul Denniston, Bonnie Dore, Mike Fierman, Jo Anne Fox Avnet, John Gallogly, Kathy Garrick, Barry Greenberg, Peter Greenwood, J.J. Hoffman, Matthew Hoffman, Erin Holt, Mary Garripoli, Neal Israel, David Johnson, Pamela Johnson, Lattice Productions, Elaine Leff, John Thomas Lenox, Marsha Lenox, Barbara Mallory, Robert Mania, Sal Maniaci, Laura Marion, Justin Meloni, Michael Petok, Marci Pool, Kelly Stables, Theatre West, and Sarah Victor. And a special thank you to Karen Lipscomb for many of the behind-the-scenes pictures.

And all the actors and crew who have worked on the myriad of Brady projects in all forms. And the Brady fans—especially the Brady fans.

—Lloyd Schwartz

PART 1

The Brady Bunch Is Born

INTRODUCTION

I've read eight books about *The Brady Bunch* written by devoted fans. That's very flattering.

However, I created *The Brady Bunch* and my son Lloyd and I produced the series. If you're looking for all the secrets about *The Brady Bunch*, you'll find them right here in this book.

CHAPTER 1

THE IDEA

One morning in 1966, I was reading the *Los Angeles Times* and I came across something that changed my life forever. It wasn't a headline; it was just an item you sometimes see at the end of a column that's not quite long enough to fill a space.

The item stated that, "In the year 1965, more than 29 percent of all marriages included a child or children from a previous marriage."

I knew instinctively that statistic was the key to a new and unusual TV series. It was a revelation! The first blended family! His kids and her kids! Together!

I knew I had to get my idea to the Writers Guild in a hurry to register this concept as soon as possible. I was spurred on by the sound of hoof beats in my head—other writers galloping along the same trail, trying to get to the Guild and stake a claim before I did.

At the time, in the mid-60s, most TV families were fairly predictable with a father, a mother, their children, and sometimes a housekeeper. Shows like *My Three Sons*, *Ozzie and Harriet*, *The Donna Reed Show*, and *Father Knows Best* had all portrayed the daily life of the traditional American family with conventional plots and resolutions. There was always a major story about the children and a subplot about the parents. But times were changing, and that one little newspaper item was all it took to provide that "Eureka!" moment that inspired me to create a new kind of TV family—a family that America was not only ready for, but maybe even needed. And I hoped that I would be the first to get the idea out there.

So I went to the Guild and filled out the paperwork with Blanche Baker, the charming woman there who always greeted each submission with a smiling, "Good luck."

I registered the idea before I even figured out any of the key details of the series, like how many children were in each of the families, or what the father did for a living, or where the families lived, or anything else about the characters or their situation.

I don't think I wrote more than seven or eight pages, including several sample storylines, for my submission to the Guild.

Several of the sample plots became episodes later on. Very briefly:

1. The oldest boy and the oldest girl run for student-body president.
2. The youngest girl could only bring one parent to the school play since there was only one ticket per child and a small auditorium. Should she bring her mother or her new stepfather?
3. The boys build a clubhouse and don't let the girls in.
4. The oldest kids babysit.
5. The family goes on a camping trip; the girls for the first time.
6. The youngest boy runs away from home because he has the mistaken notion that all stepmothers are evil stepmothers.
7. One of the kids gets measles. Which doctor should they call?

But first, I had to put a title on the series.

Because it wasn't about his kids and her kids, I called it "*Yours & Mine*." Eventually, it became *The Brady Bunch*.

This was a different kind of creation than my series, *Gilligan's Island*. In that case, I was searching desperately for an idea with great social significance, but one in which I could use broad characters to illustrate how different kinds of people are forced to live together for some reason. If people could work together during the day then go home to different houses and different circumstances, what would force these people to stay together at night as well?

In the middle of the night—actually at three in the morning—I awakened from my sleep with the idea: What if they were stuck on an island someplace, and they couldn't get off?

I was so excited with this creative solution to my problem that I woke up my wife and told her the idea. She ordered me to go back to sleep. But I didn't sleep. And that night, *Gilligan's Island* was born.

So shows get started in different ways.

As for *The Brady Bunch*, this series got started with a cup of coffee, the morning paper, and a dash of inspiration. You never know where or when inspiration will hit, and I knew from past experience that I had to run with the idea.

Now that I had my idea for a new family series, it was time for the hard part—writing the pilot!

CHAPTER 2

WRITING A PILOT SCRIPT

Writing a script for one episode of a half-hour situation comedy series is one thing. Writing a pilot script that will launch a half-hour situation comedy series is something else again. Writing an episode of a continuing series is like climbing a familiar mountain. Sure, it's always a tough climb, but you know the general direction of script-writing thanks to all the other writers who climbed the mountain and blazed the trail before you. You're also familiar with the characters and the situation of your continuing series.

But a pilot script is an entirely different kind of mountain. It's a Mount Everest kind of mountain because nobody ever climbed that particular peak. Who? What? When? Where? Why? How? The responsibility to answer these questions is all in your lap.

A lot of self-appointed experts will advise you to avoid originality when pitching a new series. A network or a production company would much rather spend their money on a proven precursor: a famous comic strip, a famous novel, a famous play, a famous song, or a hit series from another country. Starting with a proven concept always makes the decision easier. And it is also what makes so many series just like so many other series.

The truly big successes are the shows that are not like other shows. And that's what I wanted *The Brady Bunch* to be.

With the pressure off to register my blended-family presentation, I turned my attention to fleshing out that skimpy outline I brought to the Writers Guild.

And writing starts with one thing: thinking.

Writing is 95 percent thinking and only 2 percent actual writing. The other 3 percent is spent drinking coffee, opening a few packs of gum, straightening a picture on the wall, or peeing: in other words, doing everything you can to avoid writing.

Let me go off on a tangent. (See? I'm even avoiding writing this book.)

When I was in the Army in World War II, I was a writer in Armed Forces Radio Service (A.F.R.S.). After basic training, I was shipped to Hollywood, where I had to be at my post at 6:30 a.m. after roll call. Then I would go to my cubicle where I would write comedy material for Army shows with seven or eight other comedy writers in their cubicles. We wrote Army shows like *Command Performance*, *Mail Call*, *G.I. Journal*, and *Jubilee*.

These shows were done live at a CBS studio on Santa Monica Blvd. In our unit, there were producers, directors, casting directors, and actors who had, in civilian life, been producers, directors, casting directors, and actors.

Since our shows were meant for American troops stationed all over the world, our casting directors could get just about any actor to participate—like Clark Gable, Judy Garland, or any other superstars.

The recordings of these radio shows were placed on large disks (this was before LPs, or tapes, or CDs) and shipped to our troops everywhere.

I was sitting at my desk one day, staring at the wall while thinking about a script idea for *Mail Call*, when Captain Pettito came by and saw me sitting at my desk.

Captain Pettito was regular Army, not previously a writer or other TV professional, and he had just been assigned to our post. He had no knowledge about writing or writers, or Hollywood for that matter.

"I thought you were a writer," said Captain Pettito.

I said, "I am a writer."

He said, "Corporal, you're not writing. You're just staring at the wall."

I said, "I'm writing."

He said, "You're not typing."

I said, "I have to think before I can type."

I told him, "Writing is 98 percent thinking. Typing only makes up two percent."

"Don't give me that percentage crap," he said.

I don't think he believed me, because the next morning I was on K.P. duty—i.e. "Kitchen Patrol"—slinging hash, scrubbing pots, and the like with all the other writers who were also guilty of thinking.

In the end, I survived my army enlistment just fine, and even improved my writing skills in the process.

But my army days were long gone, 23 years past, when I started writing the pilot script for *The Brady Bunch*. The first draft was simply my initial point of view of this blended family, and I had to ask myself a lot of questions.

First, I had to decide how many children each parent had.

I knew one kid per parent was wrong. It didn't give me the kind of stories and fun I was looking for.

Two kids per parent didn't seem quite right, either. Not enough jealousies and frictions and problems.

Four kids per parent meant eight kids. That seemed too many to get to know in a half-hour show, which is actually only 23 or 24 minutes if you take out the commercials.

But *three* children each seemed right. Six kids would give me the kind of byplay and stories I was looking for.

That's what I decided. Three kids each.

There were also a mother, a father, and a housekeeper as part of that family—nine people in all.

Yes, a housekeeper. Early on, I decided that a housekeeper would be an important element, with six children in the house. And compared to today, having a housekeeper wasn't as unusual then as it might sound now.

In 1966, there were quite a few families with housekeepers, both in real life and in TV and radio. When I wrote the *Ozzie & Harriet* radio show in the late 40s, the Nelsons had a housekeeper. You didn't have to be a millionaire in those years to have a housekeeper.

I reasoned that when Mr. Brady's wife died a few years earlier, he hired a housekeeper to take care of his three boys when he went to work. In my mind, dad Brady was a white-collar professional, not a blue-collar worker. That also made it easier to justify a housekeeper.

Of course, these days moms are often in the workplace along with dads, sharing the burden of the cost of living. But back in the late 60s, I wanted the mother in *The Brady Bunch* to be a stay-at-home mom who took care of the six children with the help of a housekeeper. Maybe I was influenced by my own life. I was a TV writer and not really wealthy, but I had steady work and we had a housekeeper to help with our four children.

Sorry. Here's another tangent, but I think it's an amusing one.

We had lots of friends who had housekeepers. One of them, Ed James, was also a television writer. He decided to get a ping pong table for his son as a birthday gift. He went to the Broadway Hollywood, a big department store on the corner of Hollywood and Vine where he found a ping pong table he liked and decided to buy it. He took out his checkbook to pay for the purchase and the clerk asked, "Don't you have a charge account here?"

Ed said, "No. I'll pay for it by check."

The clerk said, "It's much simpler to open a charge account. Then you and your wife can use it whenever you shop here and there are other benefits as well."

Ed was reluctant to take the time out to open an account, but the clerk persisted. "It just takes a minute. Customer Service is right over there."

So Ed went over to the service desk and told the young woman he'd like to open a charge account. "Fine," she said. "Just fill out this application."

One of the questions on the application form asked who he worked for and the address of his employer. Ed said, "I'm a freelance writer. Sometimes I write a script for a show on CBS or a show on NBC. I don't have a permanent place of employment. I get paid by that particular show."

The young woman was indignant. "How can I give you a credit card when you don't even have a regular job?"

"I have different jobs from one month to another," Ed responded, "and I work at home."

Ed was a good writer and he was always in demand. He became more and more annoyed as this woman continued to ask questions. Finally, he said, "Let's just forget it. I'll get the ping pong table someplace else." And he stormed out of the store.

That night Ed was having dinner with his family—his wife and two kids. His housekeeper was serving dinner and she heard the story Ed told his family about his frustrating experience at the store. When his housekeeper heard the story, she said, "Mr. James, you could have used my credit card from the Broadway."

"How did you get a credit card?" Ed asked her.

She said, "I got a regular job, Mr. James. I work for you."

So housekeepers, in relatively middle-income homes, were not rare in the 1960s, at least not in the entertainment business.

That's why my pilot script included a housekeeper.

CHAPTER 3

AND STILL WRITING. . . .

More questions for myself.

Who was the Mr. in this family? What did he look like? What did he do for a living? Was he a widower?

Who was the Mrs.? What did she look like? Was she a widow?

Were they both divorced? (But at that time the "D" word wasn't an option on television.)

With six kids in total, how many kids did she have? How many did he have? How many were boys? How many were girls? What were the sexes and ages of the children?

I had to do some basic thinking about this family.

Does Mr. Brady have a store? Is he a doctor? Or a teacher?

He has three kids and he's about to marry a woman with three kids. He's going to have to provide for a family of six. And a housekeeper.

Is he a lawyer? A social worker? A zookeeper?

What is his background? Does he have a college degree? Bachelors? Masters? M.B.A.? What?

And a lot more questions for Mrs. Brady.

What is her background? Is Mrs. Brady divorced? Or did her husband die?

How did Mr. Brady wind up with his three young boys? Did his wife die or was there a custody battle?

I opted for him being a widower. And I opted to leave Mrs. Brady's past open. That might provide me an opportunity for future stories.

Age is another question I had to answer—the ages of Mr. and Mrs. Brady, and the ages of their children. If the kids are in a range of six to fifteen years, that would put Mr. Brady around 40 and Mrs. Brady around 35.

Did I have to establish how they met? I didn't think so. Not in the pilot film I was planning to write.

I wanted to start the script with the day of the wedding—to show the father in his home with his family, and to show the mother in her home with her family.

One thing I was sure of: The pilot would lead to a big master scene in the backyard of the bride's parents' home for the major wedding scene, the ceremony, with "Here Comes the Bride," etc. It would be a funny scene with both parents, all six kids, the housekeeper, and a dog and a cat chasing each other amongst the guests all over the backyard.

Then Mr. and Mrs. Brady would leave on their honeymoon. In fact, that was the title of my pilot episode, "The Honeymoon."

As I always did with any script, I first construct a diagram of the script which effectively helps me keep track of each character in each scene in the story.

I draw a horizontal line across a sheet of typing paper, dividing the sheet in two; a first act and a second act. Then I draw several horizontal lines to divide each act into several scenes in each act. Then I write notes for the scenes indicating where the scene takes place, who's in it, and the subject matter.

The diagram for the pilot of *The Brady Bunch* looked like this:

1st Act
Mr. Brady and his three boys at breakfast, with Alice serving them. They are all discussing the wedding later that afternoon. Mike is trying to make sure his boys will behave them-selves and act friendly to the girls. He wants them to leave Tiger at home. They try to get Tiger into the car. A cut to Carol shows the boys and Mike arriving at Carol's home. About 4 pages
Marcia, Jan, and Cindy and the nervous bride to be. The three girls telling their mother what a beautiful bride she is, and she is as nervous as Mike is. About 3 pages
This scene is only ¼ of a page, just enough to show them driving a dog to a cat named Fluffy, the cat belonging to the three girls. It's like driving a firecracker to a lit match. About ¼ page
Carol and her parents, Mr. & Mrs. Tyler, in their backyard where the wedding will take place. About 1 page
The wedding - Mike and the three boys arrive with Tiger. They leave the dog in the car, but Tiger presses on the electric release, lowers the window, and goes into the backyard. The guests start arriving and seat themselves on folding chairs. Tiger makes a beeline for Fluffy's house and scares Fluffy into the backyard where all hell breaks loose as the cat, followed by the dog, scampers across the guests and the food and eventually pulls the tablecloth holding the wedding cake. Mike manages to protect the cake for the moment, and then it falls on his face. Carol kisses the whipped cream off his face and it's a general mess. About 8 pages

2nd Act
A lovely hotel - Day - A lake or mountain in the background - Lobby Mike signs the register "Mr. & Mrs. Brady and family" - but the manager says they had requested the honeymoon suite - he's puzzled. "You did ask for the honeymoon suite?" The desk clerk is a prissy obsequious clerk. Mike has a little fun at his expense. Various cuts of Carol and Mike, without dialogue, as they try to enjoy their honeymoon in Suite H. About 1 page
Suite H - They sip some champagne, joke about effect of champagne on them and the year it was bottled, 1962, the year Cindy was born. About 2 pages
The girls have sad little faces. Somehow kids are alright now. "I bet my boys have smiles a mile wide," Mike says. Cut to Boys not eating cake, staring at cake. Over this they hear their dad yelling at them. "Those girls are going to be his favorites now. We'll get blamed for everything." About 3 pages
Cut to girls and Alice - Night - Girls' bedroom Cindy says, "And I can't help it if I scream and cry." Jan says to Cindy, "There's no use crying about it now." Marcia says, "You should try to act grown up, like me." Then she cries and screams with them. About 3 pages
Meanwhile, Mike and Carol can't enjoy themselves at the hotel and Mike says, "You know what we have to do." They put on their coats over their nightclothes and get the girls and boys to come back to the hotel with them, much to the surprise of the desk clerk—especially when Alice, Tiger and Fluffy accompany them to their honeymoon suite. About 6 pages

This diagram gave me all the "who," "what," "when," "where," "why," and "how" I needed.

Time for another tangent. . . .

There was a very talented young writer named Jimmy Komack, whom I met when I was head writer (now called "show runner") on the 1960s sitcom *My Favorite Martian*. Jimmy was gifted, but he wrote scenes that were overly long and kept going beyond their value to the story. He needed control. I told him about my "diagram" system which I demonstrated by applying it to one of his scripts.

Jimmy was really excited about my "method." He said he was going to use that on every script he wrote from then on. In fact, he asked me if he could have that sheet of paper. I said, "Sure." It was just a sheet of typing paper that I had divided into boxes like I always did.

Some eight or ten years later, I ran into Jimmy.

He said, "Just a minute, I want to show you something." And he took a folded-up sheet of paper from his wallet and opened it.

It was the same sheet of paper I had used to show him my "method" of sticking to the story.

Jimmy said, "This is the best thing that ever happened to me. It channels my work, and it's been terrific. That's how I sold two series, *The Courtship of Eddie's Father* and *Chico and the Man*."

I've shared this "method" with other writers who wrote scripts for my shows. Recently, Lloyd told me that he ran into some new writers who had taken a class in a university where their professor discussed "The Sherwood Method." The diagram has been passed along by someone and named after me. I guess fame comes in many forms—in this case, a piece of paper divided into scenes.

Back to my own writing of the pilot. After sticking to my diagram and writing and rewriting the script a number of times (2, 3, 4, 5, 6, 7, who knows?), I was finally satisfied with my TV pilot script for "*Yours and Mine*."

The next step: selling the series.

CHAPTER 4

WHAT NOW?

In those days (1966), there were only three networks: CBS, NBC, and ABC. If I were going to sell my show, it would have to be to one of them.

I already had a relationship with NBC and CBS. I had worked for NBC on a series called *I Married Joan* after my work as a radio writer. Then I moved to CBS where I worked on *The Red Skelton Show* and *My Favorite Martian* before creating *Gilligan's Island.*

But would they accept this gentler kind of comedy from me? Just like actors are typecast, so are writers.

Oh, well, no way to find out but to approach each of the networks to see who wanted to do a new kind of show about a blended family.

As I was soon to find out: Nobody. . . .

Going to CBS

I diligently made phone calls to the executives in charge of comedy development at each of the three networks: CBS, NBC, and ABC.

Even though thousands of scripts arrive each year at these networks, I had enormous confidence that "*Yours and Mine*" would become a series.

Because of my history, the first place I headed with my new TV series was CBS.

In advance of our meeting, I had sent a copy of my pilot script for "*Yours and Mine*" to Paul King, the new executive in charge of comedy development at CBS.

I also sent copies of my pilot script to NBC and ABC. But my network of choice was CBS.

When I got to CBS and met Paul King, we exchanged greetings and a few reminiscences. Then he said, almost abruptly, "Sherwood, I think your pilot script is terrific."

What a great way to start a meeting!

Then he said, "However. . . ."

("However" is the word I have learned to hate most in the English language.)

Paul's "however" meant, "However, we don't do these kinds of pilots any more."

I was honestly puzzled. I asked, "You don't do *what* kind of pilots?"

He said, "*Pilot* pilots. A pilot that tells how the series starts. At CBS, we like first pilots to be the third episode, or the seventh episode, or the tenth or whatever. We want the viewers to learn about the show whenever they tune in. If the show is written well, the viewers should be able to pick up the idea of the series from any episode."

"Write another episode," he suggested, "then we can set up another meeting and we can discuss a deal for a series. We really like this concept."

I said, "Paul, this is not your usual situation-comedy family. It's two families blended into one. Nobody has done a series about this kind of family before."

"That's why we like it," he said.

"Then why keep it a secret?" I asked. "They'll see what fresh new stories they can look forward to in a different kind of situation comedy. Unless you think exposing the idea makes this script dull?"

He said, "No, no, no. It's not dull. It's a very good script. And it's a wonderful idea for a series. We just don't do pilot pilots anymore. We like to start with another slice of the pie. Come back with another slice. Then we can set up another meeting to talk about a series."

I thanked him for the meeting, and I left, still puzzling about this "slices" business.

I remembered exactly what Jim Aubrey, the head of programming at CBS said when he called me to say he was putting *Gilligan's Island* on the CBS schedule back in 1964.

Jim said, "Sherwood, I still hate your fucking show, but the viewers love the pilot so much, I have to put it on the schedule."

No matter how crudely it was phrased, I considered Aubrey's comment a far better outcome than the meeting I just had with Paul King. Better news than, "Sherwood, I think your script is terrific, but we don't do pilot pilots any more. Come back with another slice."

That night Mildred roasted a turkey for dinner. When she served me the turkey she asked, "How many slices?" I said, "Honey, don't say 'slices.' Don't say 'slices!' I never want to hear the word 'slices' again."

Later that evening, I overheard Mildred on the phone talking to a friend of hers. "That's right. Sherwood doesn't want me to use the word ' slices' anymore."

Then she listened a moment and said, "How should I know why? He's a writer. They're different."

I was still confident I could sell my new concept with that pilot script. And there were still NBC and ABC.

Going to NBC

Since my early days with Joan Davis, I was no stranger to NBC. I hadn't created *The Joan Davis Show*, but I was head writer. I was also the writer/producer who had created *Gilligan's Island*, a very successful CBS series. And now I was approaching NBC with a pilot script for a new series I had just created.

Shortly after my meeting with CBS, I went to a meeting at NBC with Peter Robinson, who was in charge of comedy development.

Peter, with a big smile, said, "We read your script here at NBC and we love it. We think it's wonderful."

"Wonderful," I said to myself. "What writer doesn't like to hear the word 'wonderful'?"

Then Peter added, "However. . . ."

There's that damn word again! "However!"

"We only have one note," he said. Then he added, "It only affects three or four pages."

"How bad could that be?" I said to myself. "Three or four pages. The script was over 40 pages long, so what's three or four pages?"

Writers are notoriously self-delusional.

"It's the last two little scenes," Peter said. "You have to change the ending."

"What's wrong with the ending?" I asked.

"It's unbelievable," Peter said.

"Unbelievable? Why?" I wanted to know.

Peter said, "You can't have two people on their honeymoon go home to bring back all their kids to join them at the hotel."

I said, "Why not? They feel uneasy leaving their children at home. They know they'll feel better if the kids are with them at the hotel. They won't worry about the kids back home."

"I don't believe it," Peter said. "None of us here at NBC believe two people on their honeymoon would go back for their kids. Six kids," he added. "Nobody's going to believe it."

"I believe it," I said.

"Of course you believe it. You wrote it. I'm talking about the TV viewers," Peter said. "Nobody's going to believe that unless one of the kids is suddenly sick or hurt. The rest of the script is fine. Just write a different ending. The script is very funny and it's very believable until that unbelievable ending. It makes the Bradys really weird."

"I don't think it makes them weird," I said. "I think it makes them very special people."

"We think it makes them both nuts," said Peter. "We would love to discuss this pilot script again when you write a new ending. We love the concept. Then we can talk about a 13-week commitment.

Naturally, I was disappointed.

CBS had insisted on that 7th or 8th-slice approach instead of my "pilot" pilot. Now NBC wants me to throw out an ending which I thought was the best part of the script.

So I went to a meeting at ABC.

Going to ABC

In 1966, Mike Eisner and Barry Diller were joint Vice Presidents of Television at Paramount, which owned ABC. Of course, they went on to become much more important in the entertainment world. Each has become a media giant.

Mike and Barry both met with me. They said they loved the concept of a blended family, and they both loved the script. They had no "pilot" pilot problem and they had no problem with Mr. and Mrs. Brady going back for the kids on their honeymoon. They thought the pilot script was perfect—the way it started, the wedding, the honeymoon, everything.

"Finally," I said to myself, "Smooth sailing!" But Barry and Mike also had a "however. . . ."

Their "however" had nothing to do with me or my script.

Barry Diller had created the "TV movie" that year. No network had ever done original two-hour TV movies before. Barry thought it would be a lot cheaper for ABC/Paramount in the long run to make their own movies instead of renting feature films from MGM, or Universal, or United Artists, or whomever, and paying for each run.

Their "however": Diller and Eisner wanted to use my pilot film as a two-hour movie, but not as a series.

I said, "I'll tell you what I can do. I can save this thirty-minute script you love for the last half hour. I can write a first hour leading into this script and make it a two-hour TV film. I can show how this couple met, in a department store, or a market, or someplace.

"Then I can deal with problems of their courtship, dealing with the relationship with each other's kids, and problems that develop among the children. And maybe between the parents as well."

Barry said, "No, no, no. We like the script exactly the way it is. Just make it longer."

Mike agreed. "Just make it longer, Sherwood."

I said, "I can't simply make a script longer. If I add extra material to those same scenes, that will hurt the scenes. They're the right length now. That's the reason you like the script. I'll be happy to add more story and make it an hour and a half."

Mike said, "No. We don't want more story. We love the script the way it is. Just make it longer."

Barry agreed. "Right. Just make it longer."

I said, "I'm happy you both love the script but I can't stretch the scenes to make them longer. If a script is too long, it's easy to take material out to tighten a script. But adding unnecessary material will make it dull unless I add more story."

We discussed this for two or three meetings. They insisted it wouldn't be dull. To emphasize this point, they said, "We will guarantee you 13 weeks on the air if you just make this script an hour and a half long."

I said, "I'm sure you mean that, but if it comes on the air and it's dull, it will have a low rating. You wouldn't want a dull show on the air for 13 weeks and I wouldn't blame you.

"You'll arrange some kind of settlement," I said, "but I will lose the opportunity of a potential series. You like the script the way it is because it's the right length at half an hour."

Cecil Barker, my producer for many years at CBS, always used the expression, "Don't piss in the tomato juice." When I first heard Cece use that phrase, I asked him exactly what he meant. Cece said, "When you have good tomato juice, don't piss in it to make more juice. You'll just ruin the tomato juice. I oughta know. I've ruined a lot of good tomato juice in my time by trying to make a good scene last longer."

ABC and I couldn't reach an agreement, and it was the end of "*Yours and Mine*" at ABC/Paramount. Thanks to the success of *Gilligan's Island*, I had what is called in the trade "F—k you money" and didn't have to take a deal I didn't want.

The three networks remained adamant. I remained adamant. More than two years went by.

I was nervous about not selling my new series, but I was determined to stand my ground.

CHAPTER 5

YOURS, MINE AND OURS AND *YOURS AND MINE*

I realized I was taking a big chance by standing pat, but I had enormous confidence in *The Brady Bunch.*

Serendipity interceded. Remember when I told you that executives would rather buy shows that were based on some previous work, like a novel, or a major movie success, or a comic book, or even on a song like "Harper Valley P.T.A."? (Coincidentally, Lloyd and I produced the TV series *Harper Valley P.T.A.* after there was already a song and a hit movie.)

Not only do executives think it lessens the risk of failure, it also leaves them less vulnerable to criticism if the project fails. If a pilot is a big hit in another medium, it gives them "an excuse for failure." They can blame their decision to buy the show on the producer, or the writer, or the director since they had backed a "sure thing" that proved itself elsewhere.

All that said, after two and a half years of no news from any of the networks, how did *The Brady Bunch* finally get on the air?

Indeed, destiny provided the details that would lead to a deal with ABC. Ironically, those same details would also almost lead to a lawsuit.

In 1968, Paramount released a movie called *Yours, Mine and Ours,* with Lucille Ball and Henry Fonda. It was a major hit, the biggest moneymaker that year. Of course, my original title of *The Brady Bunch* was "*Yours and Mine*" and it was registered that way at the Writers Guild—"*Yours and Mine.*"

In fact, the concept of the movie *Yours, Mine and Ours* was exactly what I had proposed to ABC/Paramount more than two years earlier as the two-hour movie version of "*Yours and Mine*"—how the couple met, the problems they encountered during their courtship, and the problems that developed with two families living together with all their kids.

The Paramount feature was based on a true story about a Captain in the Navy with ten kids who married a woman with eight kids. Bob Blumofe was the producer of the movie.

Obviously, I couldn't claim his movie was based on my pilot script, because his film was based on a true story. But Mr. Blumofe couldn't claim I got the idea for *The Brady Bunch* from *Yours, Mine and Ours* because my TV pilot script was registered with the Writers Guild as "*Yours and Mine*" before his movie was even filmed.

Nevertheless, when the first episode of *The Brady Bunch* hit the air on ABC on September 26, 1969, Mr. Blumofe notified Paramount that he was starting a lawsuit against ABC and Paramount, claiming I had stolen the idea to make my series, *The Brady Bunch.*

When John Reynolds, then the President of Paramount, learned about the lawsuit, he asked me to stop by his office as soon as possible. He was very concerned about this legal threat.

I said, "John, let me dismiss this lawsuit right now."

I quickly dictated a letter from his office to Mr. Blumofe.

"Dear Mr. Blumofe," I stated, "The original title of '*The Brady Bunch*' was actually '*Yours and Mine.*' It was registered at the Writers Guild two or three years before you did this movie. You can check with the Writers Guild.

"Incidentally, '*Yours and Mine*' was the title of my series, and you called your movie '*Yours, Mine & Ours*' by adding a kid of their own. Just be happy I didn't sue you."

That was the end of the lawsuit.

But the important thing was that someone at ABC/Paramount remembered my show, saw that the successful *Yours, Mine, and Ours* demonstrated the viability of a blended-family comedy, and called me.

CHAPTER 6

PUSHING THE ENVELOPE

To demonstrate the fear that encompasses the executive ranks in Hollywood, consider this tangent:

While I was producing *The Brady Bunch*, I got a call from one of the Paramount executives who told me that Paramount had just sold a new comedy series for the upcoming fall season to one of the networks. They had a 13-week commitment.

I congratulated him. Then he asked if I would please take a look at the pilot. He would set up one of the smaller viewing rooms for me. They wanted my expertise to provide feedback on their new show.

It seemed like a curious request for a studio with a 13-week commitment. I was working on *The Brady Bunch* and I couldn't produce anything else at the same time. I wondered why they needed my opinion. But I said okay.

Then he added, "I'd like you to view this by yourself." That made his request seem even more curious.

Anyway, I went to see the pilot and called him afterward. He asked me what I thought of it. I said, "It's a funny pilot. Is there some kind of problem?"

And he said, "Not really a problem. I just have a vague feeling it could be a little better. What do you think?"

"Anything can be better," I temporized.

"Of course," he agreed. "I'm not sure it has legs."

(The phrase "has legs," in show business terms, means it's a series that could go on for years.)

I said, "Well, that pilot really doesn't have anything to say, if that's what you mean. It would be better if there were some cake under the whipped cream."

I volunteered, "*The Brady Bunch* is also a family comedy, but it's about something: a blended family. Something that's happening in our society. That gives it some significance."

"Is there any way to do that with this series?" he asked.

"You mean a rewrite?"

"No, no, no. The network loves the show just the way it is." He reminded me about their 13-week deal. "Could you make it say something without changing it?"

"Well, it's hard to change something without changing it."

"Would you think about it?" he asked. "Maybe that's what's troubling me. I guess this show doesn't really have significance."

I'm not sure he realized how difficult that might be, to do a rewrite without doing a rewrite. But he was a nice guy and I liked it at Paramount, so I told him I would give it a shot.

I went back to my office and came up with an approach. My approach didn't change the story. It didn't change the characters. It didn't even change any of the scenes. The only thing it changed was the husband's job.

I phoned the executive and told him I had an idea that might work.

He said, "Great. Can you get right over here?"

I said, "Sure." A few minutes later, I was in his office with an envelope containing my two-and-a-half typewritten pages.

"How did you solve the problem?" he asked.

I said, "It's right here in this envelope. It's only two or three pages." I pushed the envelope towards him across his desk.

Before he even touched it, he hesitated. "Remember," he said, "they love the pilot just the way it is, so I hope you didn't really change anything."

"No, I didn't change anything significant; I gave it, as you put it, 'legs'—substance."

"I don't want to look like a fool," he said. "We told them the pilot was great and they think the pilot is great also, so how can I tell them I made it better?"

I said, "Why would you be reluctant to tell them you made it better? I'm a writer. I've been trying to make scripts better all my life. That's what I think I'm doing with your project."

"Well, they might lose confidence in this show," he answered. "I told them the pilot was great just the way it is."

He pushed the envelope back towards me.

I said, "I didn't call you, you called me. You said something was troubling you. Maybe this change will make you feel better about it."

I pushed the envelope back towards him. "See for yourself."

He thought a moment and then he said, "What if I really like this change? I'd be crazy to make waves when they like it just the way it is."

And he pushed the envelope back to me.

"I can tear it up right now," I said. "But if someone told me how to improve a story or a scene or even one line, I would be happy to make the change. And I would thank him for the suggestion."

"You're right. Let me have that envelope."

I pushed the envelope back towards him.

Before he opened it, he stopped again, and said, "I'm not sure they would understand the significance of this change. It might unravel our whole deal."

He pushed the envelope back to me.

"Okay. It doesn't make any difference to me one way or the other," I said. "I just thought it would make you a real hero if you told them you improved this pilot by making a little change that'll make this great pilot even greater. It can't hurt to take a look." And I pushed the envelope back to him.

He said, "It's too chancy. We do business with the networks all the time.

So it's not just this project. Anything in the future might be at risk if I guess wrong on their reaction to this idea."

This man was truly in such agony about making this decision, I was sorry I got the idea. Without realizing it, I had placed him in the worst possible position as an executive.

He didn't care about being a hero. He was just terrified at the prospect of being wrong in the first place. He pushed the envelope back to me. I decided to put an end to this meltdown of a really nice guy and a good executive.

So I took the envelope and left his office.

That unopened envelope still resides somewhere in the clutter of unused communications and letters and scripts, plays, movies, TV shows, outlines, and rewrites, etc. in the dusty depths of one of my closets.

P.S. That TV pilot went on the air exactly the way I had seen it in that small viewing room by myself. The series aired for 13 weeks, as guaranteed, and it left without growing "legs."

P.P.S. Recently, I bumped into Garry Marshall, a famous writer/producer/director and occasional actor. We hadn't talked for some time, and we were trading odd show-business stories when I told him about the envelope at Paramount that went back and forth across the table. I didn't know that particular pilot was written by Garry. There were no credits on the film.

(Garry and I are good enough friends that I almost asked him to write the foreword for this book, but Monty Hall and I are even older friends.)

Anyway, after I mentioned the envelope incident at Paramount, he said, "Oh, my God. Why didn't you tell me? That would have made *Me and the Chimp* a great series."

Anyway, another example of two ships (or producers) passing each other in the night.

CHAPTER 7

ABC COMING TO ME

After the success of the movie *Yours, Mine and Ours*, which was released in 1968, ABC/Paramount suddenly had renewed interest in the series I pitched a couple of years earlier.

The important fact from my viewpoint was that Paramount recognized that a film about a blended family made a lot of money. This was a clear demonstration that portraying a blended family was accepted with open arms by the public. That gave the executives "an excuse for failure" in case my series failed.

Still, it was a surprise for me to get a call from ABC. After all, I had sent my new series to them over two years earlier.

From their perspective, my idea now had a track record.

Because they really wanted the series, they no longer asked me to "piss in the tomato juice," and I was free to do the show that I had written—starting with the pilot episode.

The call from Paramount gave me a 13-week commitment for *The Brady Bunch*. And they allowed me to do it the way I wanted.

Was that a good decision on the part of ABC/Paramount?

You be the judge. Excuse me for tooting my *Brady* bugle, but the following is a record of the accomplishments of the Brady franchise:

- From 1969 to 1974, the original *The Brady Bunch* anchored the successful Friday night line-up on ABC. *The Brady Bunch* was a lead-in to *The Partridge Family*, which became successful as well.
- During its five-year run, *The Brady Bunch* knocked 11 different competing TV shows on NBC and CBS off the air.
- As of 2010, *The Brady Bunch* has had all kinds of sequels and spin-offs, it has been running in syndication for 35 years, and it is still running in 43 countries.

Talk about legs. I'm proud to say *The Brady Bunch* has legs, like a caterpillar has legs!

CHAPTER 8

THE DIRECTOR

As soon as I was sure my pilot script was going from script to film, the first phone call I made was to John Rich—my first choice to direct the pilot.

John and I started working together in 1950 on the TV series, *I Married Joan*—John as a director, and I as a writer. Since then, John had become one of television's top directors, having won Director Guild and Emmy Awards for *All in the Family* and *The Dick Van Dyke Show.* I had a bit of the same sort of history. I had won an Emmy Award for *The Red Skelton Show* and several awards from the Writers Guild as well.

In addition to being an extremely talented director, John Rich was a good luck charm for me since he had been involved with my other series, *Gilligan's Island* from the beginning and directed the first eight episodes.

When I finally sold the pilot script of *The Brady Bunch* to Paramount, John was available and a deal was made for him to direct the pilot and additional episodes as well.

A financial tangent:

John later told me about a decision he made with the studio. Paramount had offered him a choice: he could receive a bonus if the pilot film became a series, or he could share in profit participation in the series. It was an either/or situation, and John had to think about his answer long and hard. He knew the television business very well.

Chances of an original comedy pilot being sold are remote at best, and chances of it lasting through the first season are more remote, and being picked up for another year are even remoter. The odds on winning a sweepstakes ticket look great in comparison.

John knew that 90 percent of the TV shows that survive in the United States are based on hit shows from England, or Holland, or other countries. John was involved with *All In The Family*. That had started in England. So had many other series.

John remembered that Norman Lear, probably the most successful comedy producer of all, with three or four major television hits, hadn't created any of them from original ideas. They were based on successful imports from England or elsewhere.

The success of *Gilligan's Island*, an original comedy series based on no prior success anywhere, was like "catching lightning in a bottle." John's phrase.

Chances of achieving that same kind of success were somewhere below nil. John had participated in the *Gilligan* success creatively and financially, thanks to a profit-participation deal he had made.

This time John took the cash bonus.

It was a very generous bonus, and John knew about studio bookkeeping and its cleverly negative affect on "profit participation." It makes Mafia bookkeeping look like child's play.

To this day, John still believes he was right in taking the bonus on *Brady*. "After all," he reminds me every time we see each other, "lightning doesn't strike twice in the same place."

Actually, statistically, lightning does sometimes strike twice in the same place. Not often, but it happens. And I was lucky enough to have it happen to me.

In any event, nobody offered me a bonus if the pilot sold, so I had no decision to make. But if they did, I would have thought it would be something like betting against myself. Let me just put it this way: I didn't even have to bet, and I won.

CHAPTER 9

CASTING THE KIDS

With John Rich aboard, we got into casting immediately, starting with the children.

Casting kids is much more difficult than casting adults. Adults usually have a body of work to help you make a decision: previous appearances on film, or TV, in various roles. So lacking useful resumes, the interviews with kids are truly critical.

I have four children of my own and that helped me. In addition, I had gone through Pre-Med and I had a Bachelor's Degree as well as a Master's Degree which included five or six courses in psychology. This all served to prepare me for the important job of casting the kids. I knew the series would eventually rest on the little shoulders of those youngsters, because most of the stories would be concerning the children's problems.

I planned to "star" a different kid in each episode from week to week. That's how I designed the series, so that meant each of the children needed to be capable of carrying the story in his/her starring week.

I spent an entire summer casting those six kids, but I didn't want typical casting: Like one overweight kid who keeps eating all the time. Or a kid who just talks about sports. Or a brainy kid who knows everything. I wanted the character of the actual child actor to be the determinant. I did have a couple of preconceived ideas. I wanted the oldest of the three boys to be a very responsible kind of boy, and I wanted the youngest girl to be cute.

Other than those factors, I wanted all the kids to be real. And I wanted their series personas to be reflective of their own real personalities. The world was wide open in terms of kids' interests, and the kids I wanted would bring their own interests to their roles.

Since it was summer vacation and kids were out of school, I could interview all day long. And I did.

To complicate things further in casting, I had to find six additional Brady kids with opposite hair colors since I hadn't yet determined who the parents would be. I wanted immediate viewer recognition with the kids and parents in terms of hair color. Blonde mother, blonde kids. Dark-haired mother, dark-haired kids. Blonde father, blonde kids, etc. No back story is needed.

As a consequence, to this day, there are three dark-haired girls and three blonde boys about 45-50 years old somewhere in the world who might have been "The Brady Bunch" kids. And they are just finding that out if they're reading this book.

In one case, I made an exception. I cast Mike Lookinland as Bobby, the youngest boy. He had kind of blondish hair, but he was clearly the best actor of the youngest boys. He was 6 ½, maybe 7. He read very well, and he was the most appealing of the boys who auditioned for Bobby.

If the boys were to be dark haired, I decided we would darken Mike's hair. That's the way it turned out. I know it was an annoyance for him and gave his hair a reddish tinge. But it instantly made him one of the Brady boys. I guess that a very early age poor Mike learned you have to suffer for your art.

Since very few young children have much experience, the casting would mostly be determined by the interviews, which were really just chats. That would make the kids feel more comfortable.

I was once asked by *TV Guide* about the number of kids I personally interviewed to find the six Brady kids. My secretary went through my files and discovered 264 interviews.

It was set up this way: I sat on a chair across from the boy or girl I was interviewing. Between us there was a coffee table. I asked the youngsters a few casual questions. "Have you had any experience in commercials, or TV, or movies, or print ads, or have you been in plays at school?" And so on.

While I was asking the kids these general questions, my coffee table served as a sort of concentration test. I placed objects on the table directly between us that might be interesting to children. There was a model fire engine, a plastic horse, a doll, and some sort of a broken object that might be puzzling to a child. I wanted to see if they would be distracted from our discussion.

On a sound stage when you're filming, there are lots of fascinating things to look at. If kids lost interest in our discussion, they might also lose interest in rehearsing. I wanted children who could stay focused. If they passed that basic test (and they were a good interview), we would move on to reading a few lines with me.

In addition to being good actors, none of the Brady kids you have been watching for all these years played with anything on the table.

For some reason, the girls were easier to cast. Maureen looked like she would grow up really beautiful, and that certainly could become part of her character. Eve, the middle girl, was very pretty but sounded like she could easily be provoked, and Susan was just as cute as can be. And she had a lisp that made her even cuter.

Barry had a sense of maturity beyond his years; Chris had a devilish side that I found very appealing, and Mike had an enthusiastic energy that made him instantly likeable.

You can understand that it has been a long time since those original interviews, and trying to remember what made each of them stand out isn't easy. I know I was taken with the ones I picked, and I dare say their lives have changed considerably because they were in my office for casting.

The one interview that does stand out in my mind was Susan Olsen's. She came in and started describing a recent role she had on "Gunthmoke." That's how she said it. And yes, the lisp was real. She told me about how she got to ride a "horth," and that there was a "thnake." She was adorable, and she got to be "Thindy" based on that brief meeting. Later, I heard that people thought that I forced her to lisp.

With Susan, as with all the kids, we just took who they were and that became their characters.

That completed our six kids in *The Brady Bunch*: Maureen McCormick (Marcia), Eve Plumb (Jan), Susan Olsen (Cindy), Barry Williams (Greg), Christopher Knight (Peter), and Mike Lookinland (Bobby).

The casting god must have smiled on me since they turned out to be wonderful choices, each and every one. They were talented, bright, and never gave us any real problems during the series. Many producers on other shows where there are children, have major problems with one or more of their kids. I was spared that difficulty.

Undoubtedly, that was because of my son, Lloyd, who started out as the kids' dialogue coach and would become the show's producer. He had been a camp counselor and he was great with kids. Throughout the series, he was on Paramount's Stage Five with them all day, every day.

With Lloyd in charge on the set, I was free to spend my time with writers and my script consultant, and in the editing rooms. That freedom allowed me to okay ideas and outlines for episodes, and to do final drafts to go to the actors and all the personnel.

Fortunately, we didn't have any difficulties with the kids' parents either. They were always on or near Stage Five in the event of some kind of emergency. The parents stayed pretty much by themselves, and all of them got along very well with each other.

With all due respect for the talents of the show's main adult actors—Florence Henderson (Mrs. Brady), Bob Reed (Mr. Brady), and Ann B. Davis (Alice)—I was sure young viewers would be drawn to the series because they would identify with kids their own age. Besides, everyone remembers his or her own childhood, so adults would watch the show as well. But in the race for ratings, I felt those kids would make it or break it.

Now that I've given gold stars to all the kids, and their parents, I must also give one to Mrs. Whitfield.

Frances Whitfield was the daily on-site teacher of all six Brady kids. I don't think we could have survived without her special abilities. She had to teach some kids at the grammar school level, and the other kids at the middle school level.

Mrs. Whitfield was determined that the Brady kids in her care would learn even more than they would have in regular classes in public schools. She gave them tests, hung their drawings and poems on the studio's schoolroom walls, and encouraged each of them to learn their school work as well as their scripts.

In addition, the State of California is very strict with rules governing youngsters in entertainment, with stringent regulations about how long kids can remain on the set, or in front of cameras and lights. Mrs. Whitfield never violated any of the state rules and regulations. She stayed strictly within those rules and, at the same time, she helped us finish the day's work on schedule.

Most people think of the *Brady* kids running up and down the Brady stairs all the time. That's what the viewers think they saw. Actually, that didn't happen very often. The six were usually only together as a group in one or two scenes in each episode. Mrs. Whitfield had her stopwatch on each of the kids checking screen time, adding up the minutes for each child separately.

The kids loved Mrs. Whitfield. Their parents loved her. Florence Henderson loved her. Bob Reed loved her. Ann B. Davis loved her. And so did Lloyd and I.

Mrs. Whitfield was a lovely lady, and I'm sorry to say she passed on in 2006. She's no longer with us but her work with those kids will remain as long as *The Brady Bunch* remains in syndication, which may be forever.

CHAPTER 10

LOOKING FOR MRS. BRADY

After I cast all the kids, which took the entire summer of 1969, I began interviewing actors and actresses for Mr. and Mrs. Brady.

Since I'm old-fashioned, I believe in "Ladies first," so I started looking for Mrs. Brady.

I wasn't looking for a real comedienne. I was looking for an actress who could do comedy to be Mrs. Brady, to share the billing with Mr. Brady and also share the screen with six children and a housekeeper.

Logically, Mrs. Brady should be in her mid-thirties in order to have children approximately 7, 10, and 13.

A major problem in casting two leads at that time of year, August and September, is that many actors and actresses in that age group are locked away by networks with "holding money" for the pilot season. Here I was in that same season looking for the perfect Mr. Brady and Mrs. Brady.

Maybe I should have looked for the adults in the summer when I devoted all of my time to casting the kids.

Nevertheless, it was now late August/September and I had to find the parents of *The Brady Bunch*. The Paramount casting department started a stream of actresses flowing to my office.

Many well-known leading ladies refused to interview. I guess they didn't want to spend screen time with six kids.

However, quite a few actresses did show up. They arrived with portfolios containing photos of themselves in various poses: a dress-up version in an evening gown, as a country girl, or in a swimsuit to show off their figure. They were the right age, but not necessarily the right talent. Many had only acted in dramas and seemed to lack a comic flair.

However, there were some interviews that were quite unusual. One attractive lady opened her portfolio and showed me full-page color photos of herself completely nude. It was pretty disconcerting, talking to her across the desk while I was looking at those pictures. Maybe she thought those photos, and all the possibilities they implied, would help her get the part. It didn't.

Another actress said she was not a good "cold" reader. She suggested that she'd be happy to come to my house to go over her lines. Or perhaps I could come over to her place and we could go over the lines together. To warm up her "cold reading?" She didn't get the part, either.

The most extreme case of I'll-do-anything-to-get-the-part was an attractive actress who said hello in a remarkable way. When I came over to greet her, she reached out her hand, and I reached my hand out to shake hers, but she reached a little lower than I did, and shook something else, and with a smile said, "Very pleased to meet you." She didn't get the part either.

For the most part, however, there were a lot of professional actresses and there were many regular interviews and readings.

One of the most professional and skilled actresses who came in was Joyce Bulifant. Joyce is very pretty and she's got a great sense of comedy.

I arranged a screen test with her and Bob Reed, a candidate for Mr. Brady. They worked well together. At that moment, I thought Joyce was the leading lady of our leading ladies. So did the executives at Paramount who had looked at the other candidates.

Another great actress, Florence Henderson, was on my wish list as well as Paramount's wish list. Early on, however, we had been unable to test Florence.

Florence had a long history in show business. She left Indiana when she was only 17. She headed for New York to join the American Academy of Dramatic Arts. A year later, Rodgers & Hammerstein gave Florence the lead in their last national tour of *Oklahoma*.

That's when I first saw Florence personally. I knew she was a wonderful singer, but I didn't realize till then that she was equally at home as an actress and comedic actress.

But Florence was unavailable. She had a regular engagement appearing at a hotel in Texas. "She will be available soon," we were told by her agent.

But soon isn't now. Our start date was around the corner, and you can't hold up shooting on a pilot film. Too many things have to come together, and the opportunity may be lost. If you wait for one piece of casting, no matter how important, it can delay you a whole year. It can even delay your pilot film forever. When opportunity knocks, you can't ask it to come back tomorrow.

We decided to go with Joyce Bulifant. Everybody agreed. In fact, I put Joyce's test and a few other tests on a short reel so the top Paramount brass could look at them, too.

The network had as much at stake in this new TV pilot as I did. Maybe more. Because if *The Brady Bunch* became a hit as an early evening series, it would help the shows that follow it on the ABC schedule.

Joyce and I, the wardrobe lady, and Doug Cramer, Vice President of Programming at Paramount, went on several shopping expeditions for casual clothes, evening clothes, as well as night clothes. Joyce was happy to go shopping, because that meant she was going to get the starring role in the show.

Then suddenly, Florence Henderson arrived in Los Angeles. Apparently, Joyce had not yet signed her contract with Paramount to star in *The Brady Bunch*. Florence's agent took advantage of this opportunity. We called Bob Reed back, who had tested with Joyce, to test the same scene with Florence.

Joyce had done a very good test.

Florence also did a very good test.

In fact, Florence's test forced us to rethink the role of Mrs. Brady, as to which actress was better for the show.

Joyce was funnier.

Florence had the ability to get a laugh but wasn't quite as funny as Joyce.

On the other hand, Florence felt more real as a wife and mother.

Did we want funnier, or did we want realer?

It was a crucial decision for Paramount and for me.

We ran those tapes over and over. It was a tough choice because Joyce and Florence were both so good.

Finally we decided on Florence.

I had to break the news to Joyce. That was tough.

We had spent a lot of time together, and now the role of Mrs. Brady was going to somebody else.

I couldn't tell Joyce this news over the phone. I guess I could have turned this task over to the casting department or to someone else, but I wouldn't have been able to sleep that night.

I went over to her house and I told her what had happened. As gently as I could.

It was a difficult cup of coffee for me and I knew it was even more difficult for Joyce.

I knew it would be quite a blow. This might be the end of a dream for her, especially if the show became a hit. In any event I knew it was a blow to her vanity. She thought she was Mrs. Brady. Joyce took the news as well as she could. I admire her. She even wished us well.

That was over 35 years ago, and Joyce and I are still friends. In fact, we worked together on another series a few years after that incident.

When Paramount and I decided that Florence Henderson would be Mrs. Brady, there was no way I could comprehend the importance of that decision.

In the first place, Florence was much better with comedy than I suspected. In the second place, she had the maturity to handle working with the very difficult Robert Reed. Much more about him later.

We were also able to use Florence's ability as a singer as the basis for several episodes. Florence is a triple threat: a wonderful actress, a wonderful singer, and a wonderful human being. And she has a wonderful, bawdy sense of humor. When Florence is in a new play and gets a bouquet of flowers and a card, she loves it when men write, "Kisses on your opening."

CHAPTER 11

CASTING MR. BRADY

Before I could cast an actor for the role of Mike Brady, I had to decide on an occupation for the Bunch's father. There had been quite a few situation comedy shows with doctors and lawyers, so I didn't want to go over ground that had been previously traveled. Dentist? No. Engineer? Maybe.

Finally I decided on "architect."

I couldn't remember a series father who was an architect. Still, an architect is a recognizable, respected occupation. Everyone lives in a house or a condominium of some kind, and everyone knows that all buildings are designed and/or constructed by an architect. Even youngsters are familiar with the word, "architect." Mike Brady: Architect. Done.

In addition, I was sure I could use that occupation as a source of stories. If the need arose, Mr. Brady could be physically involved in construction. Besides, he could be working in a firm with other architects, where he could have a boss to whom he was responsible.

Whatever Mr. Brady did for a living, he must have done it well for him to afford a nice, two-story house for his family.

In my mind's eye, I always saw a two-story house. That would be more interesting if six kids ran up and down the stairs, going to and from school. It was the picture in my head of an ideal blended family. I wanted it to be the right house in the right neighborhood, upscale and traditional, for the six kids, a mother, a father, and a housekeeper. As it has worked out, that two-story house has become as well-known as the actors.

For the role of Mike Brady, there were a number of men I wanted to interview, including Gene Hackman.

Paramount wouldn't even okay Gene Hackman for an interview because he had a very low TVQ. (TVQ is a survey that executives use to determine the audience's familiarity with performers. TV executives don't admit to the existence of TVQs, but it is commonly employed in casting.)

The year after *The Brady Bunch* debuted, unknown Gene Hackman with no TVQ starred in *The French Connection* and won the Academy Award for Best Actor, and has been a major star ever since.

Like the actresses, many well-known actors wouldn't interview. Others sent film. Paramount didn't like to judge from film and neither did I. You never know how old the film is, or whether the actor had gained or lost a lot of weight or hair recently.

Among those that did interview, who did have name recognition value, was an actor named Jeff Hunter. I really liked Jeff, but I thought he was too handsome, like a male model in shirt ads. Jeff had intense blue eyes and had starred as Christ in the movie *King of Kings*.

Jeff really wanted to be Mr. Brady. When I told him I thought he was too handsome, he insisted he wasn't that handsome any longer. He pointed out the lines around his eyes that made him look more mature now and not quite so good looking. I told him that I was suffering from the same affliction, and he laughed. Jeff had a wonderful sense of humor.

He came back to interview again. Twice. But I couldn't convince myself that he was the Mr. Brady I was looking for. I just wasn't comfortable with Jeff as Mr. Brady.

I also liked Robert Reed. Bob did some tests with a few of the Mrs. Brady candidates, and he was very good. However, there was one factor I didn't know at that time. It was a fact that made it almost inevitable he would become Mr. Brady.

Based on Bob Reed's popularity in the father-and-son legal series *The Defenders*, Paramount had made a substantial deal with Bob because he had a very high TVQ. Paramount signed an overall deal with Bob for a lot of money. It was pay or play. Even if he weren't acting on a show, they'd have to pay him, and they don't like paying people for not working. Suddenly, he was the Paramount favorite, and soon enough he would be hired as head of the Brady household.

Paramount had a number of TV pilots in the works for the 1969 season. They thought Robert Reed would star in one of them. Among those was a pilot based on a film starring Cary Grant called *Houseboat*. Another pilot was based on the film *Barefoot in the Park*, starring Robert Redford.

Bob Reed fancied himself another Cary Grant or another Robert Redford, and he was anxious to star in either of those pilots. Unfortunately for Bob, he got neither.

Meanwhile, nobody had talked to him about *The Brady Bunch*. *The Brady Bunch* was just an original script for a TV pilot by someone named Sherwood Schwartz, who Bob Reed had never even heard of. There had never been a *Brady Bunch* feature, or a *Brady Bunch* novel, or a *Brady Bunch* anything.

As it turns out, Bob really didn't want to do a show with six kids. But due to his contract, he had no choice.

It really made no difference to me whether Bob Reed had a play or pay deal with Paramount because he clearly did the best film test with Florence.

Also of no concern to me was Bob's sexual orientation. In fact, I had no idea Bob was gay until the first day of shooting of the pilot of *The Brady Bunch*.

We were filming in the San Fernando Valley on a local location in Sherman Oaks. The very first scene we filmed was the wedding scene. It took place in the backyard of Mr. and Mrs. Tyler's home. Carol Martin, their daughter (who still had her first husband's last name), was about to become Mrs. Brady that afternoon. Carol (Florence Henderson) had been living there with her parents and her three daughters.

The backyard was beautifully decorated for the wedding. Lots of flowers and white chairs for all the guests. A minister conducted the service.

The very first shot featured the minister with Carol and Mike. After the usual wedding ceremony remarks—"Do you take this woman . . . do you take this man . . . etc."—the minister, played by Dabs Greer, said, "Aren't you going to kiss the bride?"

The groom, Mike Brady (Bob Reed) said, "You bet I am," and he kissed the bride, now Carol Brady (Florence Henderson).

Right after that scene with Bob Reed, Florence came over to me and said, "Sherwood, what do you know about this guy?"

I said, "Not much. He did a wonderful test with you. That's why you're both here. Why?"

Florence said, "He's gay."

I was surprised, but I said, "Well, gay or not, he's Mr. Brady. Lots of guys in show business are gay."

Florence said, "Of course I know that. I was just surprised, that's all."

I said, "I am, too. How'd you know?"

Florence said, "I've kissed a lot of men. No straight man kisses a woman like that."

Florence and I never really talked about that aspect of Bob Reed again.

During the entire run of the series and subsequent TV movies, Lloyd and I always guarded his "secret."

The Brady kids in an early-season group photo.

The ever serious Robert Reed.

Everyone's favorite mom, Florence Henderson.

Barry Williams as Greg.

Maureen McCormick as Marcia.

Chris Knight as Peter.

Eve Plumb as Jan.

Mike Lookinland as Bobby.

Susan Olsen as Cindy.

Ann B. as cheery as ever.

Tiger . . . but which one?

COVER CALL

WA NO. 2556

SERIES THE BRADY BUNCH

PRODUCER SHERWOOD SCHWARTZ

DIRECTOR JOHN RICH

TITLE THE HONEYMOON

PARAMOUNT TELEVISION

CALL SHEET

PROD. NO. 61090-001

DAY FRIDAY, OCTOBER 4, 1968

FIRST DAY OUT OF 8 DAYS

REH. OR LV. CALL

SHOOTING CALL 8:00A

LOCATION STAGE 2 CULVER CITY

SET # SET	SCENES	CAST	D/N	PAGES	LOCATION
3- INT. BRADY BOY'S BEDROOM	16-17	1-3-4-5 (TIGER)	D	2 4/8	
4-	113 THRU 116	1-2-3-4-5-9	N	1 7/8	
5- INT. TYLER GIRL'S BEDROOM	112	1-2-6-7-8	N	1 4/8	
6-	98 THRU 101	6-7-8	N	1 2/8	
1-	88 thru 95				
2- Kitchen	2→5, 11→14, 15(PT)	1-3-4-5-9			
				7 1/8	

CAST & DAY PLAYERS	PART OF	MAKE-UP/~~LEAVE~~	SET CALL	REMARKS
1. BOB REED	MIKE	7:30A	8:00A	
2. FLORENCE HENDERSON	CAROL	9:00A	10:00A	
3. BARRY WILLIAMS	GREG	7:30A	8:00A	
4. CHRIS KNIGHT	PETER	7:30A	8:00A	
5. MIKE LOOKINLAND	BOBBY	~~7:30A~~	~~8:00A~~ 9	
6. MAUREEN McCORMACK	MARCIA		7:30A	SCHOOL
7. EVE PLUMB	JAN		7:30A	SCHOOL
8. SUSAN OLSON	CINDY		7:30A	SCHOOL
9. ANN B. DAVIS	ALICE	9:00A	10:00A	

ATMOSPHERE AND STANDINS			SPECIAL INSTRUCTIONS
1 STANDIN	WEEKLY (LEN FELBER)	7:30A	COVER SET
1 STANDIN	WEEKLY (HELEN TRUMBO)	7:30A	
2 STANDINS	WEEKLY (MIDGET)	7:30A	
4 STANDINS	WEEKLY (MINOR)	7:30A	
1 WELFARE WORKER			

ADVANCE SHOOTING NOTES

SHOOTING DATE	SET NO.	SET NAME	LOCATION	SCENE NO.
MON 10-7		EXT. TYLER'S HOUSE	4101 LONGRIDGE SHERMAN OAKS	18-19-21-22-20, 23 THRU 27, 110-34-41-42
TUE 10-8		EXT. TYLER'S HOUSE		28 THRU 33, 35 THRU 40, 43 THRU 53
WED 10-9		EXT. TYLER'S HOUSE		54 THRU 84
THUR 10-10		EXT. TYLER'S AND BRADY'S HOUSES		105 THRU 106, 1
FRI 10-11		HOTEL SUITE AND LOBBY	STAGE #3 CULVER CITY	102-103-104-107-108-109 117 THRU 125, 86-87

UNIT PROD. MGR. WALLY JAMSON PHONE 1311 ASST. DIR. Jim Myers/E. Dismukes PHONE 1311

ART DIR. BOB SMITH PHONE 1311 SET DEC. JOHN BURTON PHONE 1311

ISSUED BY OPERATIONS: DATE ________ TIME ________ APPROVED ________

MD 300-1

The first episode's call sheet.

Mike, teacher extraordinaire Frances Whitfield, and Susan in the studio school room.

Frances Whitfield after the kids had left for the day.

Cindy asking a department-store Santa for a Christmas miracle—curing her mom's laryngitis.

Dialogue Coach Lloyd with some of the Brady kids.

The Brady boys in the attic.

The Brady girls in the girls' bedroom. Notice the top of the set and the microphone.

Jan—*not* allergic to Tiger.

Ann B. flashing her brilliant comic timing.

A young Susan and Mike on a break from shooting.

Mike using Chris' back to sign an autograph.

Sherwood talking to the cast on set by the famous Brady staircase.

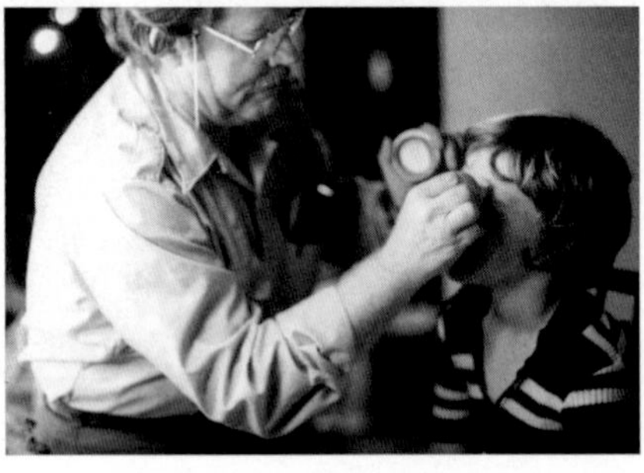

Mike getting a make-up touch up.

The Brady family on the rim of the Grand Canyon.

Mike and Eve at the Grand Canyon.

Susan and Mike signing autographs for their fans.

Sherwood swinging with Susan. The lawn was famously fake Astroturf, but the swingset was real.

Dialogue Coach Lloyd with Susan.

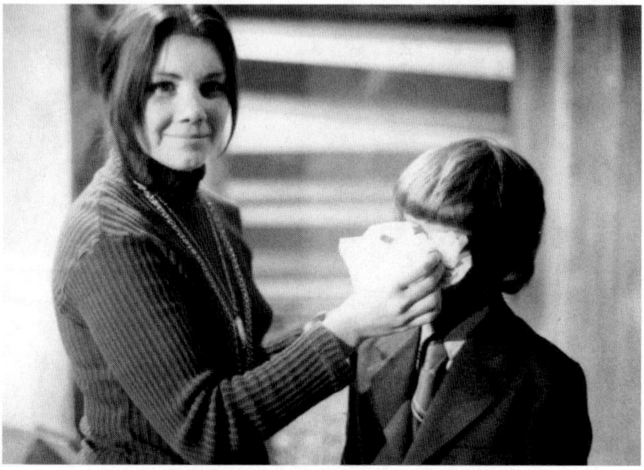

Our make-up woman, Charlene, powders Mike.

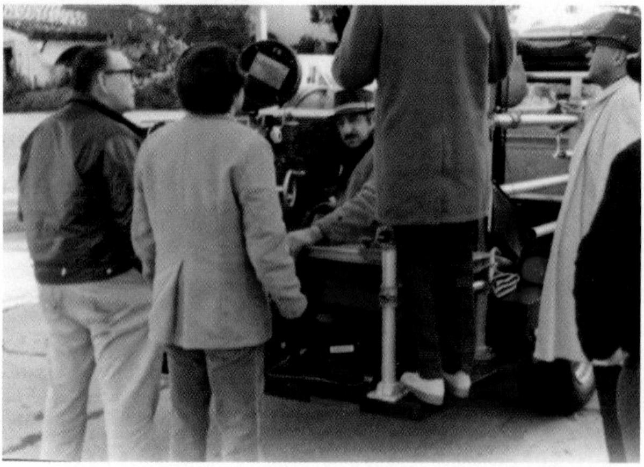

The Brady Bunch crew on the rare outside location in Hollywood.

Greg sings, "Till I Met You." Was this a foreshadowing of "Johnny Bravo"?

Mike and Carol Brady. (No, that's *not* a cell phone in Mr. Brady's hand. The series ended long before cell phones.)

The Bradys at Christmas.

More holiday cheer.

CHAPTER 12

HIRING THE HOUSEKEEPER

In thinking about Mike Brady and his sons after his wife died, Mr. Brady most certainly would have hired a housekeeper to take care of his three boys when he had to leave home to go to his office.

And Mr. Brady would have kept his housekeeper when he remarried. It would even be more necessary now because he was marrying a woman who had three children of her own.

I knew that whatever the episode, the kitchen would become a very important room, maybe the most important room in the house. Six kids would be running in and out, getting snacks, picking up their lunch bags to take to school, etc. Of course, the housekeeper would have to be a major character in the show.

When I started to cast the housekeeper, I wanted to avoid minorities. Actors and actresses of color, whether African-American, Hispanic, or Asian, have played domestics for many, many years.

In 1949, I, myself, had written a program in radio called *Beulah*, starring Hattie McDaniel. Hattie was probably the most famous housekeeper of all time. She played Mammy in *Gone with the Wind*, and she became the first black actress to win an Oscar.

I thought minorities had been typecast long enough. I wanted to cast someone away from those usual stereotypes. I simply wanted an actress who had experience playing comedy roles to share the kitchen with Mrs. Brady.

I interviewed a great many character actresses with comedy backgrounds. One of them, Monte Margetts, seemed to have some sort of Scandinavian accent, Norwegian or Danish, and I thought that she would add a little flavor to that character. Monte had played a lot of comedy and I felt secure in casting her as the housekeeper because Joyce Bulifant (before Florence arrived) could handle comedy so well.

The housekeeper was a pivotal character. She might be a confidant to the kids, since kids sometimes are reluctant to confess something to their parents directly. Parents might be able to learn things from the housekeeper. This was another reason that the housekeeper would be very important in the series.

When Florence was cast as Mrs. Brady, that change affected the role of Alice. I now knew I needed more comedy in the kitchen and felt we had to sign an actress with greater proven comic ability. Monte Margetts had never had this kind of co-starring role.

We needed . . . who? The only actress I could think of for that part was Ann B. Davis. I thought Ann B. would be perfect. As Schultzie in *The Bob Cummings Show*, Ann B. Davis was a comedy whirlwind.

ABC/Paramount immediately said, "There's no room in the budget for Ann B. Davis. She's very expensive."

"So is filet mignon," I answered. "If you want the best, you have to pay for the best."

I guess it's easy to spend other people's money.

Indeed Ann B. had won numerous Emmy awards. And there are some things money can't buy. Like love. Or talent. Talent was what Ann B. has. And love is what the viewers have for Ann B. Davis. They still love Ann B., and they always will.

I'm sure Paramount was relieved, financially, to learn that Ann B. Davis was unavailable. She was in Seattle performing a regular gig in a comedy club.

That gave Paramount an excuse to look around for a substitute, someone less expensive.

I said, "There is no substitute for Ann B. Davis."

They said, "The only way we can get Ann B. Davis is to buy out the last two weeks of her engagement in Seattle." Paramount asked, "Is she that essential?"

I said, "The success of the show may depend on it!"

I knew that with Florence and Ann B. in the kitchen, the comedy would be solid.

Paramount got the message.

Forty-eight hours later, Ann B. Davis arrived from Seattle.

I didn't know at the time what Ann B. Davis had to do to get from Seattle to Paramount for an interview. In fact, I didn't even know it till I discussed it with her when Lloyd and I started writing this book.

After *The Bob Cummings Show*, Ann B. didn't have a steady job on television, and salaries weren't what they are today. She had been working in theatre, but her savings were dwindling. She had to spend a lot of her own money . . . and then borrow money from her agent . . . just to get to Los Angeles to meet me.

It turned out to be a wise decision for her and us, since Ann B. put on her blue apron and didn't take it off for six years.

I'm sure I've made more important decisions in my life, but I think that casting Ann B. Davis as Alice was one of the biggest in the life of *The Brady Bunch*.

Ann B. is the consummate professional. She doesn't judge material. She just plays it the best she can. She has said that if the lines aren't the very best, that's the time she earns her money by making more of the script. I love her for that.

All in all, we were lucky with the cast. Florence Henderson was wonderful and a dream to work with. Ann B. Davis was wonderful and a joy on the set. The six kids were wonderful and were always willing to go the extra mile. And Bob—well, eight out of nine isn't bad.

CHAPTER 13

ALL ABOUT BOB

From the very beginning of filming, Bob Reed was reticent about the series. He objected to just about everything. When he objected to a line of dialogue, which was frequent, or even a whole scene, which was almost as frequent, I would often have to rewrite it or transfer that material to Florence and/or to Ann B. Davis.

As the series would go from episode to episode, I turned more and more to my two guardian angels, Florence and Ann B., with new dialogue or scenes to make the series work. Bob never cared about his role being diminished. He just wanted to make sure everything was real, and not what he considered "jokey."

One of our directors, Jack Arnold, who had won directing awards in America and England, said to me, "What is this guy doing in a situation comedy? He's as much fun as a temporary filling."

Bob had spent two years with a Shakespeare company in England where I guess he thought he was the next Laurence Olivier. He really wanted to be a leading man. After his role on *The Defenders* with E.G. Marshall, he landed the male lead opposite Julie Andrews in the movie, *Star*.

The movie was a failure at the box office, and Bob got bad reviews. He had to look toward TV to resurrect his career.

Bob thought television was beneath him, but his agent told him he had to face facts and forget about features after that *Star* experience.

With feature film stardom out of reach, Bob signed his overall television deal with ABC/Paramount.

At that point in his life, Bob was approaching 40 and was very disappointed in his career. He resented the idea of being the "father" of six children in a TV series. However, if he wanted his large salary every week, he had to perform his services as a co-star in a situation comedy, sharing credit with a bunch of kids.

I'm sure he resented me because I represented his failed feature-acting career.

In addition, I had created and produced *Gilligan's Island*, which Bob considered the nadir of all TV shows. If he had a punch line to a joke or physical comedy, he would often say to me, "Why don't you save that stuff for *Gilligan's Island*?"

In retrospect, I guess I should have inquired about any comedy in his background, but I was primarily looking for chemistry between Florence and Bob.

Unfortunately, the test used for Mr. and Mrs. Brady was a purely romantic scene, without any comedy, so I had no clue about his lack of comedy understanding.

However, lack of comedy instinct was the least of my troubles with Bob. Bob insisted on picayune accuracy on everything and anything. He checked every minute detail in the script with his *Encyclopedia Britannica*, which was his bible. I wasn't striving for inaccuracy, but comedy is based on the willing suspension of disbelief to make it funny, and Bob Reed wouldn't bend at all.

I'm sure Bob used to read a scene with the script in one hand, and the *Encyclopedia Britannica* in the other.

One good example of my problem with Bob was a scene in which Florence and Ann B. were each cooking strawberries in the Brady kitchen to compete in a jam contest. Bob was supposed to walk up to the entrance of the kitchen, and he was supposed to take a deep breath and say, "This smells like strawberry heaven."

When Bob got to that point in the scene, he left the stage.

I received a call from Lloyd on the set. He told me Bob went to his dressing room without a word to the director or anyone else. Of course, that stopped the shooting. The scene was lit and the other performers were in place, but Bob was in his dressing room, and Paramount was paying for a lot of wasted time.

Meanwhile, I was forced to leave my office where I was working on future scripts, or casting, or editing. I had to go to Bob's dressing room to discuss the problem. That became a frequent procedure.

The following dialogue became a virtual mantra between Bob and me during my visits to his dressing room.

I would say, "What's wrong, Bob?"

He would say, "If you don't know, I can't tell you."

I would say, "Well, let's try English."

This time, Bob said, "I'm supposed to approach the kitchen where Florence and Ann B. are cooking strawberries and I'm supposed to say, 'This smells like strawberry heaven.'"

I said, "I know. That's what's in the script."

Bob said, "You really don't know, do you."

I said, "No, I don't know. Tell me."

Bob said, "It so happens that strawberries, while cooking, have no odor, so how can I say, 'It smells like strawberry heaven'?"

I said, "Who says strawberries while cooking have no odor?"

And Bob replied, "It's right there in my *Encyclopedia Britannica*. Why don't writers and producers check these facts out?"

Bob wasn't the technical advisor on the show. He was an actor. Apparently, he couldn't act anything that wasn't accurate in his opinion.

I said, "Bob, I can smell strawberries in the kitchen, in the dining room, the living room, all over the set, and right here in your dressing room."

Bob asked, "Do you want me to believe your nose or the *Encyclopedia Britannica*?"

I didn't want to get into a discussion on that level. Time was flying away and so was a lot of Paramount's money. I tried to find a quick solution so we could continue filming.

I asked, "Can you look into the kitchen and say, 'That looks like strawberry heaven?'"

He said, "Sure, I can say that."

Bob didn't offer that as a solution. Through divine knowledge, I was supposed to channel his opinion and have it taken into account before the script was written.

The same thing happened while filming another scene, when two eggs fell out of the refrigerator and Bob was supposed to slip on them.

Again, I got a call from Lloyd and I arrived on set in the Brady kitchen. Bob was standing next to the refrigerator. Shooting was halted.

Bob said, "According to the *Encyclopedia Britannica*, contrary to popular opinion, eggs are not slippery when broken. They are sticky. Writers and producers must learn to check these things."

As Bob was telling me this, he opened the refrigerator door. Two eggs fell out. He slipped on the broken eggs and fell right on his butt.

That time he had the good grace to laugh, and from the floor he said, "I guess I deserved that."

But those kinds of incidents went on *ad infinitum.*

I guess I should have foreseen these problems right from the start, right from the filming of the pilot.

During the wedding ceremony, Bob was supposed to catch the wedding cake as it slid off the table, at the end of the dog-and-cat chase.

Bob was trying to catch the big wedding cake as it fell from the table. He tried to catch the cake and balance himself at the same time. Bob fell backwards and the cake fell on his face. When he sat up, his face was covered with white frosting. It was really funny.

Florence made it even funnier when she rushed over and kissed him, getting the frosting all over her face as well. She loved that. The guests, and even the minister, laughed.

It worked perfectly, from my point of view, and also for the viewers. We could tell it worked from audience testing.

After filming that scene, Bob's only comment to me was, "Why don't you save that pie-in-the-face stuff for *Gilligan's Island*?"

Our relationship was doomed right from the start.

I thought it was Bob's experience on *The Defenders* that caused me all the grief, because that series was strictly dramatic and now he had to do comedy. But I learned that was not the case. I had a friend who was one of the writers on *The Defenders*, and he told me Bob Reed was equally as much trouble on that lawyer show. Bob checked every word in the script against a variety of legal sources. He wanted to make sure the writers weren't deviating from actual case procedure, word for word. I guess it was just Bob's genetics. I'm sure he would have had Shakespeare doing rewrites. "A ghost in *Hamlet*? Impossible! Take it out!"

He would often resort to writing long diatribes that he would send to me, to Paramount, to the network, to anybody anywhere who he felt would see his point of view. I often would receive calls from the people who received his lengthy critiques. They didn't see his point of view. They just wanted to know what was wrong with him. He would begin his dissertations with historical explanations about the history of comedy, so as to help educate the readers of his essays about the history of entertainment. I'll spare you that part, but here's an excerpt from one of Bob's notes about a gag-store inkblot which one of the kids uses as a practical joke in an episode. This was merely *part* of a five-page rant.

"As was contended three weeks ago, the difficulty of creating a 'gag ink spot' to resemble even remotely a stain is insurmountable. In the teaser, the on-lookers are required to believe that the stain is real. Now while the metal gag 'ink spills' may be placed upon a flat non-porous surface such as a floor or a table-top, their lacquered finish shining like a wet puddle, and be remarkably realistic, the same item placed upon a piece of moving, pliant, porous cloth creates no illusion whatsoever. Anything wet would have soaked into the material and dried."

At first blush, he sounds bright and thoughtful, but we're talking about a gag inkblot—which did indeed look real. Bob's comments were based on his review of the script before he ever saw the prop. But without ever looking at the inkblot, he did seem to maintain he was an expert on gag inkblots and porous cloth. In truth, the plot of the episode came about because I used a gag inkblot when I was a kid, and my parents believed it and got mad at me. Maybe my mother and father could play it, but Bob Reed couldn't.

In spite of his antagonism for me and my scripts, Bob grew to love the Brady kids. All of them. In many ways, he treated them as though they were his own kids. He took them all on a trip to Europe one summer, and got them gifts on various occasions.

Bob saved his anger and resentment for me and for my son, Lloyd, who was the producer of the series. We both shared the brunt of Bob's constant anger and resentment for as long as we worked with him.

In spite of all of the problems that Bob caused, he provided a strong father figure for *The Brady Bunch*. The image of the father on television comedy shows has taken a beating, but Mike Brady was there for his kids offering wisdom and guidance. Robert Reed brought qualities of integrity and honesty to the role. That cannot be denied, so as much pain as he caused us, I'm glad Robert Reed was Mike Brady.

CHAPTER 14

PRODUCTION

As Vice President of Television at Paramount, Doug Cramer was my main man at the studio. In fact, Doug had accompanied Joyce Bulifant and me and the wardrobe lady on the shopping trips when Joyce almost became Mrs. Brady.

Doug was really in his element in fashion and attire. He knew a lot more about fashion styles and garments than I did, and he was always concerned about "the look" of the show.

For example, when the closet door was open in the girls' room, and the camera could see the sweaters in the closet, they had to be cashmere sweaters. Nobody talked about the sweaters. They were just there, but they had to be real cashmere. He was a stickler for classy things.

Doug and I didn't see eye to eye on details like that; but in important matters, Doug was enormously helpful.

Doug Cramer wasn't involved with casting the Brady kids or dealing with them. I don't believe he had children of his own, and kids held no particular interest for him. But he was especially helpful in pushing Paramount for extra money in making a deal for Ann B. Davis to play the housekeeper.

Another extremely important function Doug served was in my never-ending feud with Bob Reed. It would have been simpler for Doug, I'm sure, to let the producers solve their own problems with a pain-in-the-ass actor. That's what producers are supposed to do. But after a while, Bob tried to circumvent me by going to studio executives. That proved to be his undoing.

In addition to the stream of voluminous notes which Bob continued to send me—criticizing me and Lloyd, over-analyzing every script, and lecturing about the stories, or the dialogue, or both—Bob started sending copies of those offensive notes to Paramount executives Doug Cramer, Emmett Lavery, Bruce Lansbury, and Hank Coleman.

Soon enough, the ammunition Bob used against me was turned against him.

Like Captain Queeg in *The Caine Mutiny*, Bob revealed to the Paramount executives what a pedantic, egotistical, childish performer he really was. They saw for themselves how every script fell victim to his absurd criticisms and his over-thought accusations.

Just for the heck of it, I set up a "sting operation." I decided to read one script from Bob's point of view, examining every possible fact he might challenge with his ever-present *Encyclopedia Britannica*.

One such fact was in a script in which Mr. Brady wants to teach the kids a lesson for hogging the phone, so he installs a pay phone in the Brady kitchen. If the kids want to use the phone to call their friends, they have to use the money from their weekly allowance.

I knew Bob would challenge the idea of having a pay phone in a private home. I doubted it myself, but I remembered something I had read recently. Knowing Bob would check that out, I called the Federal Communications Commission (FCC) in Washington, D.C. and asked if there were any areas in Southern California where it's legal to place a pay phone in a private residence.

It turns out there's one area in Southern California where it's legal: Santa Monica.

That was what I remembered from an article in a magazine about J. Paul Getty, a billionaire whose residence was in Santa Monica. J. Paul Getty had a pay phone installed in his home so guests had to pay for their phone calls. Maybe that's how he became a billionaire.

Amazingly, because of J. Paul Getty, it's legal to have a pay phone in Santa

Monica (at least it was in 1969). Armed with that information from the FCC, I sent the script to Bob. I knew I would get a phone call, and it came immediately.

Bob took the bait.

He asked, "Sherwood, where do the *Brady Bunch* live?"

I was all sweet and innocent when I replied, "In California."

Bob, annoyed, said, "Of course I know they live in California. I can see all those palm trees in the show every week. Whereabouts in California?" he questioned.

"Southern California," I responded, innocently.

"I know that, too," Bob said, growing irritated. "Where in Southern California?" he asked.

"In the Los Angeles area," I said.

"Where in the Los Angeles area?" he persisted angrily. "Los Angeles is a pretty big area!"

"Santa Monica," I answered. "Why do you ask?" I asked, still innocently.

Bob, furious, said, "Never mind!"

That sound was followed by the slam of his phone on the receiver.

I had evaded his attempt to trap me. In fact, I had trapped him.

But Bob's nasty comments about every script continued coming to me, to Lloyd, and to Paramount executives.

CHAPTER 15

POST-PRODUCTION

Here's a brief aside to introduce some of the most important people involved in making *The Brady Bunch* series.

The unsung heroes in turning a pilot film into a series are the people in post-production. They never get the credit that is rightfully theirs.

It's obvious to a viewer what actors do. And sometimes the viewer is aware of the contributions by directors and writers that make a series come alive week after week.

Post-production people, on the other hand, live in comparative obscurity. However, they are critically important in setting the pace and the tone of the series.

For example, consider the terrific editing in the pilot of the wedding sequence. Moving at a frenetic pace from the cat to the dog to the girls to the boys, and from the guests to Alice, and from Carol to her parents, and finally to the wedding cake and Mike and Carol—the skilled editing made that scene hilarious. It could have been amusing without that crisp editing, but the editing turned it into a classic sequence.

Sometimes editors can even make something where there is literally nothing. In the episode, "Confessions, Confessions"—i.e. the one with the famous line, "Mom always said, 'Don't play ball in the house!'"—Peter feels guilty that he broke his mother's favorite vase. His brothers and sisters had confessed since they didn't want him to miss a camping trip. Peter goes to sleep, and he comes to his parents in the morning and confesses since he is guilt-ridden.

The problem for us as producers was even greater than Peter's problem. That episode came in short. We needed a minute more of film, and we didn't have the time or budget to shoot another scene.

I'm not sure whether it was Lloyd's idea or mine, but we had the film editor create a dream sequence representing what Peter was dreaming about while he was sleeping. We grabbed a shot of Peter sleeping from a different episode, and put some wavy lines over it to start the dream. Then we took the footage of the basketball breaking the vase and ran it backwards and forwards, up and back, as it smashed the vase over and over in true nightmare fashion. Thanks to the editor, we got our minute as well as one of the most memorable scenes in the whole series. And it was done without shooting any extra film!

Another time there was a production problem that was resolved with a unique solution. The Brady family was riding bicycles. A quick way to shoot that was to load the actors and the bikes into trucks and do a brief ride just outside the studio. On the day before filming, the location manager came back and reported the following problem: It was late December, and all the houses had Christmas decorations up. Since the episode was supposed to be in the summer, it wouldn't make any sense. What to do? Easy solution: A few blocks to the west was a Jewish neighborhood—no Christmas decorations—so we moved our shot there. Thank goodness there is freedom of religion in this country—and around Paramount.

I have great admiration and thanks to all the editors from *The Brady Bunch*, as well as the sound editors and music editors and sound effects editors and production staff.

CHAPTER 16

THE THEME SONG

Before a pilot film is ready for broadcast, there are two additional elements needed to finalize the film: the theme song, and the opening credits.

The first thing I did when I needed a theme song for *The Brady Bunch* was call George Wyle, who had written the music for the *Gilligan's Island* theme to accompany the lyrics I had written. George had written hundreds of songs, and I was hoping we could work together again.

However, George was unavailable since he was under contract to *The Andy Williams Show*. You may remember him from being on camera with Andy during many song numbers.

George was out, but I also knew a songwriter named Frank De Vol who had written several important theme songs for television, like *My Three Sons* and *Family Affair*. I hired Frank, and it was one of the best decisions I ever made. (Brady fans can see Frank on camera; I used him as one of the talent-show finalists in "The Show Must Go On" episode where he played the saxophone.)

Frank and I discussed *The Brady Bunch* and we watched the pilot film together several times.

I gave Frank my lyrics:

"The Brady Bunch Theme"

Here's the story of a lovely lady,
Who was bringing up three very lovely girls,
All of them have hair of gold, like their mother,
The youngest one in curls.
Here's the story of a man named Brady,
Who was busy with three boys of his own.
They were four men living all together,
Yet they were all alone.
Till the one day when the lady met this fellow,
And they knew that it was much more than a hunch,
That this group must somehow form a family.
That's the way they all became the Brady Bunch.
The Brady Bunch, the Brady Bunch.
That's the way they all became the Brady Bunch.

Frank took those lyrics and did a wonderful job with the music. His music for *The Brady Bunch* is excellent because it is remarkably adaptable as it is used in many scenes. "The Brady Theme" can be used as a romantic ballad, a march, a waltz, hillbilly, or jazz, and as most of the cues between scenes.

Based on the same surveys of television themes that made "The Ballad of Gilligan's Isle" theme song Number One, "The Brady Bunch Theme" is television's seventh-favorite theme song.

I'm amazed that I've co-written two theme songs in the top ten, and I'm not even a musician or songwriter by profession.

Lloyd keeps me humble on this point since he keeps asking what the line "They knew that it was much more than a hunch" means. What can I say? Not much rhymes with bunch.

When I was a kid, I had a brother-in-law who was violinist. He taught me to play. He was convinced I was going to become a great violinist. I knew he was wrong and so did our neighbors. As far as I was concerned, the violin and I had an adversarial relationship.

However, I retained enough musical knowledge so I can tap out a tune on a piano after hearing it just once.

In any event, I was able to tap out my version of *Gilligan's Island* and *The Brady Bunch* on the piano well enough so I could work with George Wyle and with Frank de Vol.

For some reason, I had always kept my violin with me over the years, as I moved from one house to another.

Finally, I donated it to the Young Musicians Foundation in Los Angeles. They never even thanked me for my contribution. I can only assume they heard about the sounds I made with that instrument.

CHAPTER 17

OPENING SQUARES

Figuring out an identifiable opening to a TV show is crucial in grabbing the audience. In *Gilligan's Island,* the shipwreck image is unlike any other series before or since.

I had to find the same kind of unique opening for *The Brady Bunch*. The music is catchy enough so that the audience will recognize the opening chords from another room and come running, but what would they look at once they sat down in front of the TV?

High on that list is immediate identification of the stars for the viewers. One thing viewers might not know is that the order of the stars' appearance is strictly governed by contractual agreements: First star to appear, second star, etc. The size and position of their images on the screen is also contractual.

That's why you see some stars have their names slightly over other stars, or in slightly bigger letters, or in boxes, or with "And also starring" at the end of the credits. All of those things are the result of intensive negotiations between the studio and the stars' agents or lawyers.

Keeping all those things in mind, my job was to honor those contracts and still make each actor's appearance as memorable as possible.

Florence would be in first position. That's why the song starts, "Here's the story of a lovely lady." Bob Reed would be second: "Here's the story of a man named Brady." At the end, Ann B. Davis would get special mention. That's why you see her join the cast in the middle square, along with the words, "And Ann B. Davis as Alice."

In *The Brady Bunch*, six of the stars were youngsters. I knew I needed close ups of those little faces to make them memorable.

How do I keep everybody happy, and abide by their contracts?

I spent many hours trying to draw something that would give me an answer to this problem. But I'm the world's worst artist.

One day I was doodling and drew three straight lines horizontally. Then I drew three straight lines vertically. The result was nine boxes, and I suddenly realized the six kids and three adults gave me nine equal boxes and I had nine stars on *The Brady Bunch*!

Perfect!

Except that contractually, Ann B. Davis needed that special credit.

This problem called for a meeting with the Howard Anderson Company, who had offices on the Paramount lot. They solve problems with special effects. They translate ideas and thoughts into reality. I admit freely that I'm lost when it comes to technical matters. But the Howard Anderson Company was equal to the task.

They used a then-new device called the "blue-screen process" to film each of the actors looking around from his or her individual box to the other actors. Technology is more sophisticated now, but that was the state of the art then.

They coordinated the nine boxes and Ann B.'s zooming in with the lyrics. It all came to life due to the technical skill of the Howard Anderson Company and to the patience and skill of the actors as they appeared to look at each other in sync. It looks simple enough when you see it, but it was a stressful process as it is repeated over and over until all the actors get their looks to one another exactly right to fit with the music and lyrics.

So, with theme song and opening credits completed, *The Brady Bunch* was now ready to telecast the first episode, "The Honeymoon," on September 26, 1969.

As usual, however, there was a "however. . . ."

A week before we were to go on the air, Paramount suddenly proposed that I use a different name for the series other than *The Brady Bunch.*

That was because an enormously successful feature film had just been released called, *The Wild Bunch*, and the word "Bunch" referred to a band of outlaw cowboys. That film was such a hit, Paramount didn't want the negative word "Bunch" associated with Brady.

I maintained that the alliteration in the phrase "Brady Bunch" was very important. Paramount thought so too, but they were afraid the viewers would get the idea that the show was a western or about a mob.

After kicking around title after title (like "*The Brady Brood*"), Paramount and I couldn't think of a better title. We finally agreed that the stigma, if there was one, would blow over.

Since *The Brady Bunch* has become popular, the word "bunch" has taken on a gentle connotation. The phrase "*The Brady Bunch*" itself has even come to define "a gentle blend of two families into one."

CHAPTER 18

S.S. PASSA BANANA

The pilot was filmed, edited, dubbed and scheduled to air on the ABC network, Friday nights at 8:00 p.m.

And I was ready for a vacation after working day and night for eight months.

By coincidence, my good friend, Irv Robbins, of Baskin Robbins ice cream fame, invited Mildred and me and eight other friends to join him and his wife, Irma, on a cruise through the Panama Canal. Irv was also Vice President of United Fruit, and we would be sailing on a freighter called, by our group, the "S.S. Passa Banana," through the Panama Canal to Costa Rica where it would pick up its cargo of bananas.

There were 12 of us, which is the most people aside from the crew allowed on a freighter. If there were more guests, it would constitute a cruise ship which would call for a doctor and a nurse.

Twelve people were also perfect for three tables of bridge. All of us were friends who could play bridge in the S.S. Passa Banana tournament.

We left from New Orleans with our first stop in Kingston, Jamaica. There was a brass band and a red-carpet greeting for us because United Fruit is pretty much royalty in Central America.

Our group disembarked, and we headed for a wonderful restaurant called The Blue Grotto.

On the way there, we stopped at the Jamaica Hilton for a drink. As we sat at tables in the lovely bar room, a voice came over the intercom, "Call for Mr. Schwartz. Call for Mr. Schwartz."

There are lots of Mr. Schwartzes, and nobody knew I was there. We didn't even know we would be there. But the intercom continued, "Call for Mr. Schwartz. Call for Mr. Schwartz."

Then the voice said, "Call for Sherwood Schwartz." Well, there aren't that many Sherwood Schwartzes, so I answered the call. There was nobody on the phone. Whoever was calling had apparently hung up.

I asked the operator, "Do you know who placed this call?"

She said, "A Mr. Cramer from Paramount Studios."

I had left my itinerary so Doug knew I would be in Jamaica, but there's no way for him to know I was heading for The Blue Grotto, or that our group had stopped for a drink at the Jamaica Hilton.

Due to the time difference, I called Paramount the next morning.

I had left instructions before I left California to call John Rich if any changes in the pilot film were necessary. As the director, John knew even more than I did about every shot in the pilot.

I couldn't imagine what Doug wanted. When I got him on the phone, he told me ABC/Paramount was very nervous because they were told the producer had finished the pilot film and immediately left the country.

Doug said he wanted me to come back as soon as possible.

Could this be another "However. . .?"

The S.S. Passa Banana was heading for other countries where there were lots of bananas, but no planes large enough to fly me back to L.A.

I had to wait until we got to Galveston, Texas. Then Mildred and I could leave the group and fly back to Los Angeles.

We left the rest of the group two days later. The others continued on to New Orleans.

As soon as we arrived in L.A., I phoned Doug and asked him what happened. Doug said, "ABC/Paramount decided to view the pilot after all, with John Rich, and they loved it. They didn't want any changes."

It turned out to be a false alarm.

I said, "That's great, Doug, and I'm delighted.

"But I'm mystified. I don't know how you figured out how to reach me. I wasn't staying at the Jamaica Hilton. We were heading for a restaurant when you happened to call. How did you figure that out?"

Doug said, "That was easy. Wherever you're staying in Jamaica, everybody stops for a drink at the Jamaica Hilton."

I guess it's like, in *Casablanca*, everybody stops at Rick's.

It must be that kind of resourcefulness that made Doug Vice President of Television at Paramount. Doug went on to be one of the producers of *The Love Boat* for many years. He had a longer cruise than I did.

CHAPTER 19

WHEN YOU'RE A HIT

Lloyd will cover most of what occurred during the actual series and beyond in his part of this book, but there was one unusual event that happened while *The Brady Bunch* was still running in prime time that I'd like to talk about.

In 1973, ABC was not even a full 24-hour network. There was a non-commercial gap between 12:00 noon and 1:00 p.m.

ABC had tried everything to fill that commercial void. They had tried news shows, soap operas, specials, unsold pilots, everything. But nothing worked.

ABC felt embarrassed as a network not to be a full 24-hour network, like their competitors, NBC and CBS. In addition, there was all the lost revenue for that hour.

One day, in a meeting on this subject at ABC, this problem surfaced again. One of the executives said, "How about stripping episodes of *Brady* in that spot every day? We have enough episodes now."

Well, nothing else had worked, and *The Brady Bunch* had a big share of core women viewers, and at that hour, many women were home.

Nobody in the meeting could remember if any show had ever been on in prime time and also stripped across the board in reruns at the same time. Would that exposure hurt the prime time ratings?

I guess ABC decided it would be worth the risk.

It worked!

ABC became a full 24-hour network.

And *The Brady Bunch* continued in prime time.

No matter how you slice it, *The Brady Bunch* has had a remarkable history.

It was an original pilot film based on no precedent when it became a series. It was finally canceled after a five-year run in prime time, with 117 episodes.

It is still in TV syndication after 40 years, and is currently running in 43 countries. In Germany, it's called *Three Boys and Three Girls*. Perhaps it has other names in other countries.

In 2007, *The Brady Bunch* was still so popular, it received TV Land's Pop Culture Award. And that's all a result of the fans' love for the show.

When I meet a new couple for the first time and they each have children from a previous marriage, very often they tell me, "We're like *The Brady Bunch*, if you know what I mean."

I say, "I oughta know what you mean because I created that show."

They don't believe me at first, but when I convince them, they often comment that the show has had an impact on their lives.

I continue to receive fan mail from all over the world asking for pictures of the cast. Some fans want a picture of me as well because they've been watching my shows for many, many years, and I guess they want to know what I look like.

Part of my office is like a post office, with fan mail coming in and cast pictures going out.

One day, in my mailbox, there were requests for cast photos from five different foreign countries: England, Australia, Germany, Ireland, and Norway. That's the most requests I ever got in one day's mail from that many countries.

I once got a fan letter during the first or second year when the show was on in prime time. It was from a young girl who said she was leaving her home in Ohio and coming to California to join *The Brady Bunch*.

That really made me nervous, especially when I got two or three more letters from other places, saying the same thing. It was a girl each time. I could tell where they lived because their return address was on the envelope. I quickly wrote to the girls' parents alerting them to what their daughters had said. I didn't know if it was an idle thought or a real possibility.

These "runaway" letters continued to come in, always from girls.

I finally made copies of my letter to parents, so I could send it out as soon as one of those kinds of fan letters arrived. Sometimes they addressed the letters to Paramount, and Paramount sent the letters to me. Other times, they somehow got my address. The last thing I wanted was to be responsible for runaway girls.

Thank goodness none of them ever showed up.

One of my favorite fan letters was a postcard. It was obviously from a very young boy, maybe five or six years old. It was printed with a heavy red crayon. It simply said, "I LIKE BRADY. I LIKE GILLIGAN. SEND PICTURES."

Occasionally, I get letters from priests or ministers or members of other clergy because they like the moral lessons and sentiments that are often the subject of stories in *The Brady Bunch*.

Sometimes members of the clergy ask me to give them a topic for their sermons.

Interestingly enough, I also get letters from prisoners in jail. They ask for cast pictures of *The Brady Bunch* to put up in their cells. They say it reminds them of happier days when they were young, before they got in trouble with the law.

One inmate wrote a second letter because someone had stolen the pictures I had sent him. He had them up on his cell wall. He figured out it must have been a prison guard, because nobody else had a key to his cell. Apparently, the guard was also a Brady fan.

Here's one last story about recognition.

One weekend my wife and I went to Las Vegas and I forgot to take pills

I need for a condition that regulates my heartbeat. Believe it or not, my particular heart condition is called, "Bradycardia." That's the medical term.

Bradycardia!

It's not named after my show. It's the medical name of my heart condition, and the similarity is just a coincidence.

The second day without those pills I had a reaction. My wife and I rushed to the hospital in Las Vegas. We went to the emergency room. One of the ER nurses came over to check me in. When she looked at the plastic wristband with my name and other information, she must have recognized my name since she turned and made an announcement to all the other ER nurses. "Hey girls, this is the guy who created *The Brady Bunch*!"

Then she lifted her arms like a band leader, and she led all the nurses in the ER as they sang the *Brady* theme song, as if they had been rehearsing together all week! They got every word of the lyrics right.

Then they all went back to their respective duties.

I just laid there for a moment, reflecting on this "performance."

A young ER doctor arrived, took my history, and ordered those pills for me.

Bradycardia! Truth, indeed, is stranger than fiction.

CHAPTER 20

AND NOW FOR THE REST OF THE STORY

You have just read the true story of how *The Brady Bunch* became a television series.

My son, Lloyd, will now continue the story of what happened during the day-to-day production of *The Brady Bunch*, and also what happened after the original run of the show ended. If you think the first part of the story was a revelation, just wait until you read the rest!

Take it away, Lloyd.

PART 2

Making *The Brady Bunch*

INTRODUCTION

A book with two introductions, two dedications, and two sets of acknowledgements? Probably a first, but why not? Dad and I have been the first to do a lot of things. We were the first, and as far as I know still the only, father/son writer/producer team in TV history.

There have been many books about *The Brady Bunch*, but in Dad's part and now in my part we thought we'd clear up some misconceptions and reveal some things that have never been told before. It was fun remembering many of the events; it was painful remembering others.

Over the years, *The Brady Bunch* has been criticized for being an idealized family, with many saying that families aren't really like that. Maybe other families aren't like the family that *The Brady Bunch* represents, but mine was. Granted we weren't a blended family, but the values expressed by the parents on the series were pretty much the same as the way my brothers and sister and I were raised.

Many times I hear the term "Brady Bunch" used as an adjective—not just referring to blended families, but to how a family should behave. How does that make me feel? Kind of proud.

Now here's more of what happened.

CHAPTER 21

WHY?

I didn't know much about *The Brady Bunch* when Dad asked me if I'd like to visit the set in early 1969. He was in the process of filming the pilot, and I was far removed from working with him. I was at UCLA and had a lot more on my mind than network TV. It was the 60s, and I was politically involved, as was everyone. At the time he was filming, I was part of a black/white comedy team: Carruthers and Blood. "Blood" was a Black Panther. We did radical humor and were thrown out of most of the clubs in Los Angeles for being too controversial.

When I showed up on location in Sherman Oaks in the San Fernando Valley, I was brought back a few years to when I had worked with Dad briefly on *Gilligan's Island*, and a short-lived series about cavemen called, *It's About Time*. At that time my job was a dialogue coach. The function of a dialogue coach on a show about cavemen primarily is to make sure what grunt to grunt and when. Joe E. Ross and Imogene Coca were the caveman husband and wife, and working with Imogene was a delight. Her comedy timing was completely unique. Joe E. Ross began his career as a baggy-pants vaudeville comedian who then starred in the TV series, *Car Fifty-Four, Where Are You?* His trademark "Oo-oo" translated perfectly to caveman dialogue. The show only lasted a year, and I left the soundstages to go to college at UCLA.

In addition to my comedy team and working on Dad's previous shows, I also had written for the popular TV show *Love: American-Style* while in college.

So when I arrived at *The Brady Bunch* location and saw the cameras, crew and actors all working, I felt comfortable, like I was returning home. Dad introduced me to the kids and Florence and Bob and Ann B. It seemed like a nice show, and I thought that would be my last connection with it.

At the time, I was starting graduate school at UCLA, all in preparation for continuing a work path away from my father. We have never had a problem in our working relationship—or personal relationship—but I thought it would be healthier if I embarked on a career that wasn't in his shadow.

The Brady Bunch was picked up as a series—how and why Dad has covered in the first part of this book—and now the series (and this book) would begin to involve me.

All of my thoughts of an independent existence evaporated in one conversation with Dad. After he told me that his pilot was going to be a series, and I congratulated him, he asked me if I'd like to be the dialogue coach for the six kids.

I immediately told him "No" since I was sure he was only offering me the position because I was his son, and I told him that.

Dad accepted my refusal and, innocently enough, asked what kind of a person should be the dialogue coach for his new series. I began to list the qualifications of the kind of person he should be looking for.

I said, "Someone young."

He said, "You're young."

I said, "Someone who has worked with kids before."

He said, "You ran a summer camp."

He didn't have to remind me that I had spent the previous two summers and weekends working with kids of all ages at a camp in Malibu.

I said, "Someone who has been a dialogue coach before."

He said, "You were."

I saw where this was going.

I said, "Someone who has had performing experience and a degree in English."

He said, "Well, you have done both of those things."

He was right. I had. I seemed to fit in every way. Dad said that there could be nobody more qualified. Besides, I had experience living with and working with Dad and already knew how he worked and how he wanted to run things. I made the decision to join him in working on *The Brady Bunch*. It's a decision that I have never regretted making. That isn't to say I haven't wondered what my life would be like if I had chosen to take a different path, but who doesn't?

CHAPTER 22

HOW?

The Brady Bunch was not my concept of a family show. I grew up on *Father Knows Best* and *Leave It to Beaver*. Those were family shows and classics. When we started work on the second episode, I thought what we were doing would be a nice show. That's all. It was nothing that I anticipated would leave a mark of any kind.

I arrived on the set the first day and met everyone again. They didn't remember me from the pilot, so I was a bit of an interloper. Though my job primarily was to corral the kids and get them ready for any scene they might be in, I first introduced myself to Bob Reed and Ann B. Davis.

Florence would join the filming in a few weeks, as explained a little later.

Ann B. never knew it, but part of the reason for her casting was my enthusiasm about her when Dad mentioned that she was available for the role of Alice. I was a real fan of her role as Schultzie in *The Bob Cummings Show*. I said to Dad, "Take her. Don't look anywhere else. She's great!" It meant buying her out of her contract, but she was worth it. I thought so, but it wasn't my money.

Then I met Bob Reed. I had urged Dad not to cast him. I wasn't opposed to Bob because of his talent or anything I had heard about how difficult he was. I would only learn that later. I didn't like him as an actor because of the shape of his head. I know that's a dumb reason, but the back of Bob's head goes straight down to his neck without bulging out. That bothers me. Okay, I know I shouldn't discriminate because of head shape, but I do. That's the same back-of-the-head shape that Spiro Agnew had and look how that worked out. Silly, huh? But it was just unnerving to me. I saw the screen tests for all the possible Mike Bradys, and I much preferred Jeffrey Hunter.

I've seen trivia on game shows that says Gene Hackman was a favorite for the role. Dad says that he couldn't get the studio or network interested, but that Gene Hackman was his first choice.

So we were stuck with Bob Reed, mostly because Bob had a pre-existing series deal with Paramount. As my side of the story goes on, Bob Reed becomes the only aspect of *The Brady Bunch* that I didn't enjoy. Other books, magazine articles, and TV movies have chronicled the difficulties that Robert had with us, the show, and with his own life, but I'll try to be fair—much as I'd like to shout invectives.

Since Florence wasn't on the set yet, the next people I met with were the kids, their parents, and the school teacher/welfare worker, Frances Whitfield. Dad cast each of the kids well as people. Who the kids really were was how he wanted to cast the show. Making them into actors would be my job.

When I finally met Florence, I was excited since I am a big fan of Broadway shows. It used to bug my fraternity brothers since their stereos were always blasting the Beatles or the Stones, and I'd be playing an original cast recording of *The Man of La Mancha* or *West Side Story*. Of course I knew who Florence was. I had seen her in *The Sound of Music* some years earlier. Florence is justifiably proud of the fact that she has portrayed Maria in *The Sound of Music* more than anybody else, including Mary Martin and Julie Andrews. In meeting Florence, I was first struck with how small she is—and how attractive. Anybody who meets Florence develops a crush on her, and I joined that club.

These were the three adult characters of the series, though my job (at that point) was to be responsible for the kids.

Most written presentations for TV shows have character breakdowns.

Dad's presentations are similar, except for the young characters in this show, and rightfully so. Dad felt that the kids should bring their own personalities to their roles. That would make them more at ease on camera. As the series would go on, we would write for who they really were and let their characters and their real personalities blend. Even today, if you ask any of them to discuss their characters, they will confuse the characters with who they are as people.

One by one. . . .

Barry Williams (Greg) was the Brady kid with the most acting experience, which makes sense because he was the oldest. His age was about the only pre-set bit of character. The oldest kid should be a leader. In Barry's own life he was the youngest of three boys. Maybe that's the reason Barry always had the desire to be older than he was. He was 14 at the time. I was 21. He wanted to be 21, and in a lot of ways I wanted to be 14. Actually, I've never found any advantage in becoming an adult. Barry and I kind of met in the middle, and I was more like an older brother to him. To the other kids, I was kind of an uncle. Barry's formal education was cut short by his work as an actor, but that didn't stop him from exercising his extensive inaccurate vocabulary. Imagine someone mixing up words like "infantile" and "infinitesimal," and you'll get the idea.

Next was Maureen McCormick (Marcia). No doubt she was and is beautiful. Maureen has always had the same face. She won a Baby Miss San Fernando Valley contest, and if you saw the pictures of her when she was a one year old, you'd see the same face she has now, and the same face she had when we all came together for filming. I was taken with just how feminine she was, even fragile-looking, so I decided to dispel any separation between her and the other kids by immediately (and intentionally) nicknaming her "Mo." Nothing is less glamorous than the name "Mo." She is still called that today by those of us who knew her when.

Chris Knight (Peter) was the one with whom I most identified. He plays the middle boy on *The Brady Bunch*. I'm a middle child, as is Chris in real life. Chris is a carefree guy who rolls along getting along. He's instantly likeable and the guy you'd want to hang out with. Of the kids, his parents (Willie and Ed) were the only true political liberals, as I was, so with everyone else I had to be more careful about discussing the direction of the country.

An odd bit of aside trivia: The length of time *The Brady Bunch* was on the air directly corresponded to the length of the Nixon administration. The difference is that we didn't go off the air because of scandal or threats of impeachment. . . .

Eve Plumb (Jan) is closest to the character she played on the show. With doting parents who were forever intimating she was more special than the others, Eve arrived with a standoffish attitude that led to many of the storylines that had Jan not wanting to be part of the group. Even today, she resists being thought of as one of *The Brady Bunch*. I like Eve, but, in my opinion at least, sometimes she makes things more difficult for herself than they have to be.

I didn't know that Mike Lookinland (Bobby) had so little experience as an actor when I first met him. He seemed like the consummate professional and had the most fun on the set. He was always crawling around everywhere and wanted to know about everything. No wonder he has gone on to work behind the scenes as a cinematographer.

And as the cute little blond girl, Susan Olsen (Cindy) was most unlike the character she portrayed. The lisp was real, but there was, and is, far more to Susan than the dialogue she said as Cindy. Susan at six was more like a peer of Maureen or Eve. I nicknamed her "The Sooze." I thought it would give her more substance and reflect on her determination. Asking "Where's the Sooze?" gives somebody more weight than asking "Where's Suzie?"

The parents for each of the children were stage parents, and as such, were used to studios trying to make them scarce. We changed that. We wanted the kids' real parents to be an extended family of the Bradys, to be part of what we were doing. I solicited their opinions since they knew a lot more about child-rearing than I did. They hovered close to any scene in which their children acted, and we welcomed that.

I developed a close relationship with all of them. I realized just how close when, after one weekend, Barry's mother, Doris, asked me, "How's your love life?" Not even my own mother ever asked me that.

Most of the fathers worked, and we would see them less frequently, but the mothers were a solid unit. Flora Plumb, Eve's mother, was the most doting and she would often run into scenes just as the camera was about to roll to give Eve's long, straight hair one last brush.

Mike's mother, Karen, was the youngest and we were practically contemporaries. Just as I became an uncle to the kids, their mothers became older brothers and sisters to me.

One other person on the set who I bonded with was Frances Whitfield, the kids' teacher. She was a southern lady and one of the finest women I ever met. She was the perfect combination of teacher/welfare worker/fan/and child advocate. Frances and I developed a close friendship.

Rules for the length of time children can film on camera are strict, and often I was instructed by the production department to distract Frances so we could squeeze out an extra few minutes of filming with the kids.

A typical conversation:

"Frances, they want me to snow you while they try to squeeze in a last shot. They want me to make up some excuse to take you off the set so they can finish the scene."

"Do they really need it?"

Sometimes they did; sometimes they didn't. Half the time I would say, "Yes, it would be really helpful."

Then she would say, "Okay, but be finished soon."

Or I would say, "No, we can pick it up later."

So she would say, "I'm pulling the plug."

There was no way I could ever snow her, nor would I try. *The Brady Bunch* went over our shooting schedule only once in five years. We were always under budget. I'm proud of that, and I think much was due to the kids being prepared and the strength of Frances Whitfield.

I'm even more proud of a different record of accomplishment. A number of child actors on other shows have had major problems outside the show. Some have been arrested for one crime or another—some crimes with serious consequences. And one little girl had even committed suicide.

None of the Brady kids is dead, a prostitute, or in jail. Sure, they've had some problems—even some serious problems—but not of a fatal or criminal kind. And much of that was because of the ambience on the set as created by Frances and, I'm vain enough to say, me. I think we created the best, most humane, and most effective way to do a show.

According to his mother, at the same time Mike Lookinland was offered the part of Bobby Brady, he was offered the part of Eddie on *The Courtship of Eddie's Father*. With advice from his parents, he picked *The Brady Bunch*, because they all felt that it would be a healthier atmosphere for him to be around other children and not be the only child on a set of all adults. I think they were right. The shared experience of all six kids gave each of them people their own ages with whom to relate. They all went through the same unique experience of being famous and on a TV show.

So the kids were presented to me. The first director, a bull of a man named John Rich, gave me simple instructions: "I want the kids to know what to say and how to say it."

How I accomplished that would be left to me.

CHAPTER 23

GETTING STARTED

Of course helping the kids to remember their lines was the practical part of what I had to do. I decided to make it all fun. I reasoned that if they were enjoying themselves off camera, we could just continue that attitude on camera. And it worked. From the very beginning there was a lot of laughter. Florence had four children of her own and they quickly became friends of the Brady kids. Siblings of each of the Brady kids were also welcomed into our growing family. My own sister, Hope, became a friend of Maureen's, as did Susan's sister, Diane and Mike's sister, Therese.

The kids would bounce between the schoolroom and the set. It was before walkie-talkies were commonly used, so I often would find myself running to summon the kids before any scene they were in. Normally that is the second assistant director's job, but I happily volunteered. I could use that time to rapidly go over the lines with the child actor one more time before he or she reached the shooting set. This quick review came after working with them on their lines when they got to the stage in the morning.

The Brady Bunch was filmed on Stage Five at Paramount. Rarely did we leave that building. Even the backyard was inside, and there was a lot of kidding among the cast about the plastic grass in the backyard. One time a large overheated light fell on the "grass" and melted a small crease in it. The solution? Leaves were carefully positioned on that patch. The first law of TV:

It's not what things really are; it's what they look like.

The schoolroom was an unused dressing room in an enclosed alleyway off the stage itself. Mrs. Whitfield brightened up the room with drawings that the kids made. Mrs. Whitfield assumed control of the alley as well. As the years went by, many fans would send in their small school pictures in fan mail they'd write to the kids in the cast. The six Brady kids pasted these pictures all over the alley, and cheery smiling faces lined what had been a grim passageway.

Just inside the heavy stage door was a cyclorama of a blue sky and trees which was used as a scene backing. Unfortunately, it didn't reach to the ground, nor was it so high that you could walk under it without ducking. The two-by-four that held down the backing was head height, and many of us at one time or another accidentally banged our heads on it when we didn't duck low enough. Everything was a game, so we would put a check mark each time we knocked into it.

The only ones who could walk under it without bending down were Mike and Susan. In the third year of the show, Mike finally grew tall enough to bang his head, and he was thrilled and proud to add a check mark the first time it clunked him.

Since the Brady kids weren't schooled actors, I would give basic acting instruction along with making sure they knew their lines. We would look at the script and I would ask them to explain why their character was feeling what he or she was feeling. I also was given the freedom to change lines when it wasn't the way a kid would say them.

The Brady Bunch was shot as a one-camera show, which means it was shot movie style. Most of the comedies today are shot on tape or film in front of live audiences, but our shows had many small scenes and had lots of close-ups. If you study the episodes, you'll notice many more close-ups of the kids in the first years of filming. The reason? The kids weren't accomplished actors and we could always work with them in close-ups until they got the line "right." That often meant my giving line readings.

Actors don't like getting line readings, and I don't like to give them. Giving a line reading means telling the actor to say it exactly as someone tells them to, and requesting that they parrot it back. The actor becomes a puppet, and it takes away his or her creativity. At the beginning I violated the "no line reading rule" since the kids often were lost on how to say a line and there wasn't enough time to coax it out of them.

My practice of giving line readings ended about 10 episodes in. I was called to the office of the president of the studio; that's like going to the principal's office. What had I done? Once there, he told me that he was pleased with how well the kids were doing, but he wanted me to stop giving line readings. It wasn't that he objected to how I was working with the kids. It was that all the kids were starting to sound like me. I cut it out, though for some egocentric reason I liked the way they sounded.

Working with the adults was a different experience. It was in the very first scene in the first episode that Ann B. Davis was in that we discovered our own special communication. Ann B. was doing a scene in the kitchen where she was stirring a pot on the stove, and I was off camera. She did a funny take in rehearsal, and when the director adjusted the lighting and her stand-in took her place, she walked over to where I was standing and asked what I thought.

I told her I thought it would be funnier if she stirred faster and faster as she got more and more interested as the discussion she was listening to got faster and faster. I was in my early twenties, and a real fan of hers, and I was shy in giving advice to this comedy superstar. She looked at me, really looked at me for the first time, and said, "You know, don't you?"

By "You know, don't you?" she meant that she felt I was someone who could help her know if what she was doing was funny. I was proud that she trusted me. And so for the entire history of *The Brady Bunch* and all its incarnations, all Ann B. had to do was look at me, and with a little gesture, I tried to help her out. Annie and I have remained close friends all these years.

Florence has had so much experience, and Carol Brady is such a good fit for her, that she didn't prepare very much except for learning her lines. She was always happy to rehearse with the kids. When she wasn't, she would needlepoint and take care of her many activities. In real life, Florence is also a little bawdier than is Carol Brady. She would come out with things that Carol would never say, and the crew loved her for it.

Working with Bob Reed was an entirely different and difficult experience. He was never casual and always carried himself with an air of superiority. He saw himself as a "great actor," and finding himself in a sitcom with six kids and a dog was not how he saw his career going. Just saying "good morning" to him was awkward. He took an instant dislike to my father. Dad's earlier hit show, *Gilligan's Island*, was physical comedy that Bob thought was beneath him. Bob was irked by the fact that he found himself in a show whose creator might infuse *The Brady Bunch* with that kind of comedy.

Dad has a good sense about what is right for one show and what is right for another. His career encompassed all kinds of comedy, from Bob Hope to Armed Forces Radio to *I Married Joan* to *The Red Skelton Show*. Each kind of show determines its own kind of comedy, but Bob Reed was supercritical from the very beginning.

Much has been made of Bob Reed's sexual orientation, but that had nothing to do with the antagonisms that grew from the beginning. Show business is an oasis for many gay men, and I have always found little discrimination because of a man or woman's sexual choices.

Bob just didn't get along with my father, and he had little use for Sherwood Schwartz's son on the set. He was snide from the outset, and that attitude sometimes would become written diatribes that were sent to anybody who would read them. He wasn't subtle about his antipathy on the set, though he reserved his outbursts for when the kids had left. It was hard for me to hear him say things in front of the camera which were openly disparaging of my father.

I talked to Dad about it. I needed to know how my father wanted me to handle a situation on the set when Bob would curse him out publicly (and often on camera). Dad said that my job was to get the show done. That was the important thing, and he asked me to not say anything. It was very difficult because I am not generally shy about letting my feelings be known. I had a meeting with Florence who was also having difficulty acting with a man who was openly hostile to the executive producer and me. Florence didn't agree with Bob's views about the show, but she knew she had to keep acting with him as husband and wife. I told her it was simple. Just agree with him. We knew and were happy with how she really felt, but it would make her life easier if she just went along with his complaints.

Bob had the respect of the kids. He always waited until the end of the day, and they had left, before he morphed into the man I learned to dislike intensely. I always wanted to shake him and say, "Bob, Mike Brady is a nice guy. People like him. Why don't you just be like Mike Brady?"

CHAPTER 24

AND THEN. . . .

What made the beginning episodes of *The Brady Bunch* even more difficult for the six kids was Florence Henderson's absence during the first six episodes after the pilot. Florence was cast in the series at the last minute and had a prior film commitment in *Song of Norway*. Not only did we film the first six episodes without her, she had to wear a wig until her hair was right for the show and matched the pilot.

Later on, Florence's hair would be her own and would change as styles changed. Personally, I liked the ski-jump mullet best.

To clarify how the first episodes were filmed with Florence in absentia: Her scenes were filmed later and edited in. It was not unprecedented. Fred MacMurray wasn't around for most of the scenes in *My Three Sons* and came in for a concentrated time and did all his scenes for the entire year. Still, for a new series starting off with six kids, this kind of filming created some confusion adding to the natural confusion of getting a new series off the ground.

For many people, the Brady series is used as an example of an ideal family. It is often satirized as such, but the Brady family isn't a nuclear family; it's a blended family. As Dad points out, the first blended family on television. He decided that the first six episodes would be stories that pointed out the difficulties of forming a family with people who have to learn to adjust and make compromises. After that, the show would be stories that would happen to any family.

Forcing people into a locked environment causes conflict, and conflict creates stories. This is why an architect like Mike Brady would design a house with one bathroom for six kids. Nothing makes conflict like fighting over who gets to use the bathroom.

Of course since the show was filmed according to 1960s television codes, there was no visible toilet in the bathroom. If that were known, the kids probably wouldn't have been fighting quite so intensely.

Dad reasoned that each child would be identifiable to a segment of the audience. Therefore, stories were created that featured a different child on a rotating episode every six weeks. It was seldom that stories were developed for the parents or Alice. It became apparent early on that it is pretty easy to get parents involved in their children's problems, but pretty difficult to have children influencing their parents' problems.

Another reason for creating this kind of structure was our quick acknowledgment that Robert Reed just wasn't funny. He played a good solid father figure and was a competent actor, but he couldn't carry any funny scenes. He was always demanding that the script become real, and therefore more serious. Besides, with six engaging colorful kids, the less screen time we spent with him the better. Also, Mike Brady, a traditional 9 to 5 working father, wouldn't naturally be home much of the time. Most of the episodes went along with the kids relating to each other and their mother and Alice. Every time Bob would enter and offer his "Hi, Honey, I'm home!" I would think to myself, "Fun's over."

The standard Brady episode would have a teaser. That's the short scene before the first commercial in which the main problem is revealed; or not revealed. Sometimes a child would come running in and say, "The worst thing in the world just happened to me," and go running out. What? We'll have to wait until the first commercial is over to find out. Or, the child will say that he'll never speak to one of his brothers or sisters ever again. What? Why? We'll find out after the first commercial. You get the idea.

The first scene after the first commercial would have an explanation and an introduction of the subplot. Subplots always involved either (1) a child or parent whom the main plot wasn't about or (2) the whole family. Then the rest of the first act has the plot and subplot escalating until the next commercial where the initial problem gets even worse. The second act keeps both plots going until they come together and affect each other. If you think about your favorite episodes, they can be viewed in the context of the formula. That's not to say the layout is mechanical and inartistic. It's just the way this series worked best.

Here's an example:

Marcia wants to join an exclusive girls club. Meanwhile, in the subplot, Peter builds a volcano for science class. When Marcia brings the girls home in order to impress them and gain membership, Peter's volcano erupts all over the snooty girls and ruins Marcia's bid (which, of course, turned out to be a positive thing).

That particular episode—Season 4's "Today I Am a Freshman"—is an example of a good messy way that plots and subplots come together.

After the body of the show, there is a short tag scene that usually is a joke about the subplot. For example: Alice falls in a dunking booth. Or the Brady family comes back from a school production of *Romeo and Juliet* where Peter accidentally yelled "Hark!" before Jan said "Who goes there?"

My working with the kids was a full time job that extended off the set. I felt that the child who was featured should have a session with me the night before the episode would begin filming. I would go to the child's house, and we would discuss the episode. I was like a tutor. But I also had another motivation for my diligence. At that time, I was unmarried and could use a good meal. The mothers of the Brady kids were all good cooks, and I got well fed once a week.

CHAPTER 25

FIRST SHOWS

Other books have been written about *The Brady Bunch*—ironically some by "experts" who weren't there and had no real inside knowledge (though they claim to know the truth). Even Barry Williams, in his successful book, *Growing Up Brady*, purports to explain exactly what was going on from the beginning. In deference to Barry, who is a friend of mine, he wasn't there either. He was a kid and an actor in the show, but he wasn't involved in why we were doing what we were doing. Barry only learned later through interviews for his book about the decisions that were made, the things that happened and how they happened. When I see Barry and we talk about *The Brady Bunch*, he'll relate something that he was told happened, but not by me. I tell him that's not what happened. He says, "Yes, it is. It's in my book."

I tell him, "Just because you wrote it down, and it's on paper, doesn't mean it's the truth."

This book has my best recollections, colored by the intervening years and the fact that I am the hero of my own life.

I won't try to do an episode-by-episode account. That has been done in other books about *The Brady Bunch*. Instead, I hope to give some inside bits of information that haven't been revealed (accurately or inaccurately) elsewhere.

Most of those who have done our series from the beginning think of those first six episodes as a unit. First, they were all directed by John Rich. Second,

Florence joined us at the end of the six and we went back and filmed all of her scenes. Third, we were all getting to know each other. And fourth, the storylines (as explained earlier) were all about trying to blend the two families.

We were filming one of the shows when the prop men brought out some signs or posters made by the studio sign shop. These were signs that the kids were supposed to have made themselves, but naturally they couldn't help but look like they were made by the professionals who made them. That's one thing that always sticks out on a TV show. I asked Frances Whitfield if the kids had arts and crafts. She said they did, and I asked if they could make things for the show when things were supposed to be made by the kids.

I didn't want to take work away from the people in the Paramount sign shop, but I wanted the artwork that is supposed to look like kids did it to look like artwork that kids do. In the same way, I got the kids involved in decorating their bedrooms on the stage.

In a later episode there was a subplot about redecorating, and I asked the girls to pick out the wallpaper. They did, and I caught hell from the cinematographer since Maureen, Eve, and Susan had picked out a design that was hard to shoot. Bob Hager, the cinematographer, asked me to change it to something less extreme. When I went back to the girls and told them of the cameraman's request, they were hurt. I had asked them for their opinion, and it didn't seem to matter. I went back to the cinematographer and asked if he could live with it. He grumbled, but he reluctantly agreed.

Any of the people who work on a show are mostly concerned with their own areas. That goes for camera, sound, wardrobe, everything. As a producer, you have to take into account what is best for the whole show. In this case, the feelings of the cast outweighed a bit of camera difficulties.

In an episode toward the end of Season 1, Mike and Carol change roles to prove a point. Mike would help in the kitchen with the girls, and Carol would help coaching baseball to the boys. We were filming a scene in the backyard, and Florence was unhappy with her wardrobe. She felt that, if she were playing with the boys, she should be wearing an appropriate shirt. She was right. The wardrobe people, who saw Carol Brady as a bit of a fashion plate, had dressed her in one of her designer blouses.

In the rehearsal, I could see that something was bothering Florence. I asked her about it, and she explained what the problem was. They were about to roll camera, and Florence really didn't like the blouse she was wearing. She should be wearing one of her husband's shirts. She started eyeing my shirt and asked if she could borrow it.

I immediately took off my short-sleeve blue plaid shirt—literally giving her the shirt off my back—and handed it to her. I stood there bare-chested while they filmed the scene. I was really uncomfortable. I asked the wardrobe department for a T-shirt, and they got me one. At the end of the filming that day, I asked for my shirt back. They told me they couldn't do that. My shirt was now officially part of Paramount wardrobe and might be needed if there were retakes. I never got it back. It is now residing in the bowels of the Paramount wardrobe department. Every once in a while, I think I spot it in a Paramount television show.

Sadly, one more unique event happened during those first episodes. The Brady series was to have been the story of a father, mother, six kids, a housekeeper and a dog. The dog, Tiger, was a sit-com sheepdog—a little too traditional for my taste. In the first episodes, he was part of the getting-used-to by the girls.

Tiger would only be brought in on the days he would shoot. In the fifth episode, Jan was sneezing and everyone thought she was allergic to the dog. Maybe this was foreshadowing of many stories where Jan didn't fit in. Anyway, it eventually comes out that Jan is allergic to Tiger's flea powder. But at first, the Bradys thought they had to give Tiger away due to Jan's allergy. There is a heartfelt sequence that has each of the boys saying good-bye to Tiger. The dog was placed in the boys' bedroom set, and I retrieved Mike Lookinland from the schoolroom. Bobby Brady was ready. The dog was ready (so I thought) and the camera rolled. The director said, "Action!" And the dog promptly ran off the set.

Dogs aren't people. They are entitled to an aberration. The trainer put the dog back on the set. Same scenario. After the dog ran off again, I went to the trainer.

"What's with the dog?"

The trainer then said words that you never want anyone to say in any situation, especially not when the lights are on and you're filming an expensive network TV show.

"I was afraid of this," he said.

"Tell me."

"That's not Tiger. Tiger was home, and he got out. He was hit by a car and killed."

I was taken aback. "That's terrible. I'm really sorry."

"Me too. He was a good dog."

Then I realized that if this dog wasn't Tiger, who was it?

I asked, "Then what dog is this?"

He confessed, "I didn't know what to do, so on the way in I stopped off at the pound and. . . ."

"You put an untrained dog in the center of a set and we're filming?"

"I was hoping it would work."

The costliest time for any production is shooting. All the salaries and equipment add up to thousands of dollars an hour. And we were depending on an untrained dog to stay. I looked around for Larry Milton, the key grip who always had a hammer ready.

"Larry. . . ."

He came over.

"Larry, nail the dog to the floor."

Before you report me to the SPCA, Larry and I both knew I didn't really mean put a nail through the dog's paw. Larry carefully put a nail through the dog's collar, and we filmed the tearful good-byes.

If you see the episode, you'll see a dog with his chin on the floor looking forlorn. A nice bit of dog acting, but he was probably just sad that he couldn't lift his head. Trust me: No dog was hurt during the filming of that episode.

This was the last episode *that* Tiger was in.

CHAPTER 26

FLOYD AND THE BUSH FISH

They were kids. Sure, they were actors. Sure, America took them into their hearts. Sure, they have become idols. But most of all, they were kids.

And I made sure they would always be kids first. After that, they could be actors or celebrities.

Because of my prior experience working with kids, I made it summer camp for these six. And it was summer camp with awards and ceremonies and legends. I began to give funny kinds of awards after a day's filming: "Person who filmed the most scenes in one take," "Person with the funniest goof-up," etc. I did everything I could think of to make it fun.

I told them that Paramount had been underwater at the time of the dinosaurs and there were still prehistoric animals that managed to survive. Underneath the windows on the Brady house exterior were plants, and I got Susan and Mike to believe that this was the home of the dreaded "bush fish"—a legend that would last the entire series.

I also convinced all of the kids that I had a twin brother, Floyd. Pardon my vanity, but I used to say to them that "Floyd is very handsome, and we're identical." Using a literary reference I borrowed from *Les Miserables*, I told them Floyd was in prison for stealing a loaf of bread. Whenever one of their birthdays happened, Floyd would always get them a present, and I never would. Floyd Schwartz was just that kind of guy.

Continuing the ruse, one time I went so far as to wear shades, comb my hair differently, and allow myself to be seen at the commissary on the other side of the room to prove Floyd's existence. It remained a game that lasted for a couple of years. Even today, when we get together, the "kids" will ask how Floyd is doing. Sadly, he is still unparoled.

This was the late 60s, and relationships between children and adults were more formal than they are today. When I grew up, I would never call an adult by his or her first name, and that's how it was on the set. I made sure that all adults were called "Mr." or "Mrs." I didn't want the Brady kids to become buddy-buddy with the crew members who were much older. I was the only one they would call by his or her first name.

When you see an interview with an adult actor who is talking about a child actor, often the adult actor will declare proudly about the child: "He's (she's) not a child; he (she's) an actor." I feel exactly the opposite. By allowing children to behave beyond their years, you deprive them of their childhoods. It turns the world upside down, and they begin to make decisions that only adults should have to make.

When Barry reached 18, he earned the right to call adults by their first names, and he had a sense of graduation and felt he earned it.

Keeping the Brady kids kids, led to my second run-in with the studio president. Once again I was summoned to his office.

"I have some reports that the Brady kids are running all over the lot."

"That's right," I said.

"Also, they've been climbing in the skywalks and using the swing set as a swing set. That's stage dressing; not for them to play with."

He went on, "Those kids are very expensive property. They could get hurt. That would delay filming."

He had referred to them as "property." That got my back up, and it was more than I could bear.

"They are not property. They are kids. And that's what people at home enjoy watching: Kids acting like kids. I don't want them to break their arms, but that's what kids do. They need the chance to break their arms. And the swing set. Show me a kid who can pass a swing set and not swing on it."

He looked at me. I was openly defying him, and studio presidents are not used to that.

"Let me get this straight: You're not going to change how you are encouraging them to behave?"

"Fire me if you want to, but I want them to be kids first. That's what's best for the show."

He was stunned that I would boldly stand up to him when I walked out of the office.

I didn't think I had overstepped my position. I was young, and I really didn't understand studio politics. It's probably because I was still in college where we learned to question authority. I stopped into Dad's office on the way back to the set.

Dad wanted to know where I had been. I recounted what had transpired in the studio president's office. Dad looked at me with a touch of alarm.

"Lloyd, I never would have done that."

"But did I do the right thing?"

"Yeah, but I don't know if I would have handled it that way."

I don't know if there were any discussions between Dad and the studio president to save my job, but nothing else was mentioned about how the kids were "running wild," and I was left to determine (and encourage) their off-screen antics.

CHAPTER 27

PERSPECTIVES

After John Rich finished his six episodes, and Florence returned, we started to have a variety of directors. Many of the situation comedies today use one director for an entire season, but that wasn't the way it was done when *The Brady Bunch* was in production. My dad felt having one director, the actors get used to a style of direction, but with multiple directors, there is an infusion of new energy. Also, new directors learn how things are done from the people who are constants, and they would often turn to me to learn inside information about the actors.

I had advice for them about Florence: Push her. Florence is so inherently good that she'd have a tendency to ease through a scene. That would be okay, and her performance would be good. But if you'd ask more of her, you'd get more from her, and that always would make a better show.

One director was working with Maureen, and there was an emotional scene in which Maureen cried. The director was thrilled with himself, that he was able to get Maureen to sob. Those of us who know Maureen didn't have the heart to tell the director that all you have to do is say "cry" to Maureen, and you'll get buckets.

One of the first directors who came on the show after John Rich was Oscar Rudolph. He was a cherubic man with a ready laugh. He was an old-timer whose experiences in show business went back to when he was an assistant director to C.B. DeMille.

The day I met Oscar, he took me aside.

"Lloyd, you're new in the business. Let me give you some advice. If you remember this, you'll go far. If you forget it, you'll have a lot of trouble."

Obviously, I was anxious to hear it.

He stated it simply: "Never ever trust an actor."

I like actors, have a lot of friends who are actors, have even married an actress, but I have never forgotten Oscar's advice. It helped me get through years with Bob Reed.

After the first six episodes, Bob Reed's behavior was clearly established. He was in a perpetual state of grumpiness, and often the directors would pull me to a corner to ask if they'd done anything to deserve his wrath. Usually, I would try to make it seem as if it were nothing to worry about, but early on, I knew Bob and knew he'd be festering until he'd explode.

It was in one of the episodes that Oscar directed, when I saw how vicious Bob could be for the first time. After the kids had left for the day, he was doing a scene he didn't like. No news there, since he was always doing a scene he didn't like. I have trouble remembering a scene he did like. Up until this moment, Bob had always been cold to me, but cordial enough. Just after the director called "Action," Bob looked in the camera and said, "Sherwood Schwartz, I hope you fry in hell for making me do this scene."

Bob knew that after each day's shooting, the film is sent to the lab where it is developed and then sent to the studio executives and network executives. He knew by attaching his attack to the film, the executives would then be treated to his hostility. When Bob said that, I didn't know what to do. Everyone on the set knew that I, besides being dialogue coach, was Sherwood Schwartz's son. They peeked looks at me to see how I would react. I was controlled enough not to run in front of the camera and deck Bob for his insulting callous behavior. That really would have given the executives something to look at. Instead, I did my job, and waited for the scene to be over. I didn't say a word and left the set. I found a niche outside where I could be alone. I cried. I had so much bottled up inside me that I had to let it out.

My dad has spent over 50 years of his life writing comedy of every conceivable kind from wit to farce, from verbal to pantomime, from monologue to dialogue, from situation comedy to light comedy to dark comedy, and had won five Writers Guild Awards and an Emmy Award, and this sanctimonious fool says things like that about the man who made him one of the stars of one of my dad's two iconic TV series. This was more than I could stand and made me want to puke.

After I regained self-control I vowed that I never again would let myself get affected by the horrid behavior of this man. I guess this is what Oscar meant when he said, "Never trust an actor."

Bob Reed always claimed to be fighting for realism while he railed against Dad's instinct for comedy. He thought these two things were mutually exclusive. They're not. Bob would often turn to the encyclopedia and find some obscure fact that, if used, would be sure to make a scene more realistic and incredibly dull. Robert was hired as an actor, not a fact checker. All we wanted Bob to do was act the role of Mike Brady. Instead, he would spend his time sending ever increasingly long memos condemning the very show in which he was contracted to act.

My dad likes to say, "Every new TV series should have its own individual 'voice:' Like a chef who serves the same stew every week that his customers love, but they add a pinch more of this ingredient or that ingredient to keep it interesting. A comedy script should be witty or satiric, broad comedy or farce, but like the chef, it should vary just enough to keep the show fresh. The same formula with a few little surprises along the way, so they recognize their favorite show and still appreciate the little differences. If you want something that's absolutely identical, buy toilet paper."

I have made a rule for myself in casting a show: Cast for nice. If you have to spend years with people on a series, don't cast people you don't like. If you do a one shot—like a TV movie or a feature film—the time you will spend with anyone is finite. You can live with a prima donna or a Bob Reed for a few weeks, but he gave us five years of unpleasantness. I cannot remember ever having a kind discussion with him about anything.

Each Christmas I would make a particular point of giving presents to the cast that reflected *The Brady Bunch*. One year I had special sweatshirts made; one year I had basketball jerseys; one year I had stationery. I perversely delighted in giving Bob these presents. He had to thank me, but I knew he didn't want anything about Brady in his house. That gave me a holiday spirit.

One year for Christmas my dad gave each member of the cast and a few others important to the show (me included) a very special black lacquered box he had ordered somewhere. These were gorgeous, thoughtful presents with the "famous" picture of the cast on top. Dad specifically didn't give a box to Robert Reed who made it clear incessantly how he didn't like the show. Some time later, Dad happened to be at Bob's house for some reason, and he saw one of those beautiful boxes sitting proudly on Bob's desk. How did it get there? Whose was it? Did he have one duplicated? Dad never asked. Bob never said. It will remain a mystery forever.

One of the complaints levied at *The Brady Bunch* was that each episode was neatly tied up in 22 minutes. People would say that's not how life is. That's a pretty unfair accusation. Are television shows supposed to be life? Think about any of your favorite shows. If the number of strange occurrences happened in real life like they do on *Desperate Housewives*, the entire street should be sealed off. On *Murder: She Wrote*, Jessica Fletcher should have been arrested just because of the coincidence of her being nearby when hundreds of killings occurred. Is *Seinfeld* or *Third Rock from the Sun* real? No. We're all just television shows.

The Brady Bunch was more real than most. In fact, many of the plots and subplots came from my own family life. Our family is not a blended family, but I grew up among four children who have had various things happen to them. We've always had a housekeeper. No one like Alice, but Masako, our Japanese housekeeper, was one with whom we could talk about our problems. So when people level the criticism that *The Brady Bunch* isn't real life, I have always been quick to say, "It may not be your real life, but it is mine."

CHAPTER 28

KAPLUTUS

Stand-ins (or "doubles" or "second team") are people who are the same height and coloring as the stars and, after rehearsals, they move onto the set where the cinematographers use them to adjust the lighting.

Our adult actors pick their own stand-ins, but the children also needed stand-ins. The state law requires additional teachers if there are more than six children in a production. This would mean that these stand-in children would be subject to the same labor laws, and we could only use them in limited hours. The obvious solution was to have small adults as the stand-ins for the Brady kids, and since some of the children were only six or seven, very small adults would be required. Frankie and Sadie Delfino, a married couple of little people, were the stand-ins for the Brady children the entire five years of the series. Frankie told me he had met Sadie when they were both Munchkins in the classic movie, *The Wizard of Oz.*

They became family, and Frankie was an unofficial host on the set. One time, a visiting six-year-old child went up to the 60-year-old Frankie. The child was Frankie's size and asked innocently, "Did your mommy bring you here, too?"

In the third year of the series, I was notified by the production office that we had to fire Frankie and Sadie. The kids had grown much taller than they were.

Out of the question. Besides being hard workers, they were part of the spirit of the show. There had to be a solution. The grips, who also liked the Delfinos, fashioned little steps made of foam and plywood and put rope handles on the sides. When "Second Team!" was called by the assistant director, Frankie and Sadie would proudly carry their portable steps into the set and stand on them to approximate the height of the kids. They had different boxes that, when added to their own heights, were the heights of the different kids. By the last year of the series, some of the boxes were almost as big as they were.

Occasionally, Frankie and Sadie would be extras in the series, but one time they made on-screen appearances in featured roles.

It was in the episode, "Out of This World," in which Greg fooled Peter and Bobby into thinking they saw a UFO. There was a dream sequence about flying saucers and aliens, and Frankie and Sadie were given green make up and space suits. When they descended from the space craft, Frankie, ever the gentleman, offered his hand to Sadie and ad-libbed, "Come on, Honey." It wasn't exactly what an alien would say, but it was adorable and we left it in.

In the same episode, real astronaut James McDivitt appeared as a guest star. We had a man on our show who actually had been to the moon. We thought that was great. He told us that his kids were so pleased that he was on *The Brady Bunch*. Now he was a real hero at home.

I guess it's all about perspective.

CHAPTER 29

ANYBODY FROM *THE BRADY BUNCH* CAN LEAVE

As we started the second season, Dad was involving me more and more in other aspects of the show. One of the first was a meeting with the people from Program Practices. Most people are unaware, but many different departments at the studio and network are involved in making sure that a show goes on television in exactly the right format and with exactly the right subject matter.

The programming department would give us format changes as to length of time between commercials. For example, a teaser should be between one and two minutes. The first act has to be between 10 and 12 minutes. The second act a little shorter, and the tag scene should be between one and two minutes. The whole show has to be an exact length to the second. In those days, the episodes had to come in at 22 minutes and 10 seconds. In addition, the tag shouldn't have any plot developments since tags are often removed when a series goes to syndication.

The meeting we were about to attend with Program Practices had nothing to do with the length of the show. Program Practices were the people involved in censorship. Certain words can be said; certain words can't. Certain body parts can be seen; certain ones can't. Things have loosened up a lot since then, but many shows—especially dramatic ones—provided challenges for the Program Practices department and the creative teams on series.

At Paramount, all of the series met with Program Practices in a meeting at the beginning of the year. When I first started working, I had just been in college and I thought a studio lot was like a campus. I believed all of us would have studio spirit like school spirit. But, in truth, studios are just a lot of different shows on the same lot. We never saw each other and only came together once each year when the word was handed down as to what we could or could not show in our series.

I was looking forward to this meeting since Dad and I were representing *The Brady Bunch*. Producers from *Star Trek*, *Mannix*, *Mission: Impossible*, *The Odd Couple*, etc. were all there.

We all sat in different pockets around the room. I was waiting for a litany of suggestive themes and words that we would be instructed to avoid. The man made a few introductory remarks about all working together to make the best television. He said he was our friend and not the enemy. It was getting to that moment that other producers saw as infringement on their creative voices.

But Dad and I never got to hear the instructions.

The man said, "Before I begin, is there anybody here from *The Brady Bunch*?"

Dad and I raised our hands.

"You can leave," he said.

We did.

Apparently our show was so innocent that he didn't think there was anything he could tell us that we hadn't already self-censored.

In the history of *The Brady Bunch*, we only had one warning on a final script. The episode was about Marcia learning to drive. She was nervous, and her Brady parents advised her that if you think about people in their underwear, they are less intimidating. In the script it said that Marcia looks at the driving-test official and imagines him in his underwear, which we would shoot for comic effect.

The censor read that and his note was: "When you film the man in his underwear, make sure he's in boxers, not in briefs."

In five years, that was our only censorship advisement, although one other time Dad was expecting a major battle.

He had submitted a script about the health hazards of smoking. Season 2's "Where There's Smoke" is the classic episode in which Greg got caught with a pack of cigarettes in his jacket pocket. This was a pet topic of Dad's, as his father died of a heart attack after years of smoking, and his older brother and his sister died of emphysema thanks to smoking. At that time, networks derived a big percentage of the money that filled their coffers (coughers?) from cigarette companies. To our amazement, that script passed without a single note from the studio. As far as we were aware, we were the first family series to deal with that topic.

CHAPTER 30

MOVING ALONG

By the beginning of the second season, things were moving along in a pretty organized manner. Dad likes calm, and aside from some Bob Reed flare ups, episode piled upon episode.

The question at the end of every season for every series is: Will they pick us up or won't they? With *The Brady Bunch*, that question was never easy to answer. Contrary to today's memory, *The Brady Bunch* was never a major hit during its network run. We were never even in the top 10. We only achieved real popularity when the series went to syndication.

Luckily, we were picked up for the second season, and I suggested some changes to Dad about the format of the show. But first, I wanted to talk to him about me.

He knew something was up when I asked for a formal meeting at his office.

"Dad, I can do more than be a dialogue coach for kids."

"Like what?"

"I can be associate producer."

Dad thought about it and said, "You're really good as a dialogue coach, and if I made you associate producer, I would lose a good dialogue coach."

"I'll still be the dialogue coach for the kids, but I can do the other job. I've been watching the associate producer, and I think I can do it every bit as well, if not better."

Dad turned me down.

"I can't do it. I just can't."

At the moment, I was unaware of the politics involved. It was one thing having his son working on the show, but to elevate me to associate producer at 23 would be blatant nepotism, even though he knew me well enough to know that I wouldn't ask for something I couldn't deliver.

"I'll tell you what," he said. "I'll make you production associate."

"What does that mean?"

"It means you'll do all the things an associate producer does, except I won't call you that."

I agreed. At least it was a step forward.

And I had ideas. First, since we were now sure that the kids had become the focus of the series, I thought we could change the song to reflect that. The original song had been sung by a band called The Peppermint Trolley Company, and I thought the kids should sing it themselves. It would be friendlier. And at the end of the opening song, they would sing, "That's the way *we* became the Brady bunch," instead of, "That's the way *they* became the Brady bunch." I thought it would be more engaging, personal, and welcoming. It was important that they sang it like kids—no harmonies and a little bit off-key.

The second change was to the bumpers. Bumpers are at the end of the episode when a deep-voiced announcer usually says, "*The Brady Bunch* will be right back." I thought it would be warmer to have our cast members say that. Both of these suggestions were accepted and led to some repercussions.

When we showed up to record the song, the music recorders and representatives of the Paramount music department were perplexed. I hadn't engaged a singing coach, and they knew that the kids weren't singers.

"That's right," I said. "I don't want the singing to be very good."

This was an anathema. "Why would we want it 'not very good'?"

"Because that's how kids sing," was my answer.

The kids also resisted; they wanted to be professional. But I won out. And

I'm glad. It just sounds like kids singing, and each year we would re-record it—and thankfully, each year they weren't very good.

As for the bumper voice-over, I thought my request was smart, creative, and cute. Hearing Cindy say, "*The Brady Bunch* will be right back" fits with the show. Paramount thought it was brilliant economically. When an announcer does the bumper voice at the end of the show, the man has joined the cast, gets paid, and receives a residual each time the show airs. That's money out of Paramount's pocket, and above all studios don't like money coming out of their pocket. With cast members recording bumpers, they are already being paid. I apologize to the baritones who lost some money, but you have to do what's right for the series. That's the number-one rule.

Since that time, many of the bumpers on various series are voiced by cast members. I guess I was a trend setter, but that was never the motivation. Again, I was trying to do what was right for our series.

So now I was "Production Associate," and as such I was at the beck and call of another Brady producer, Howard Leeds. Howard had worked with Dad before, and he was an instrumental part of the success of the series. But Howard was an only child and never had children of his own. He had a particularly difficult time relating to the six kids, and they were never very fond of him. Fortunately, for all concerned, he had left the kids to me. But now my other duties put me more in contact with Howard.

I was in the office on a non-shooting day when he said to me, "Could you run a looping session in a half hour?"

I said, "Sure."

What Howard didn't know was that until that moment, I had never heard the term "looping." All of my time had been spent on the stage. When he asked me, my choice was simple. I could say "What's a looping session?" and then he'd know he had a production associate who wasn't up to the job. Or I could say what I said: "Sure."

I left the office and found the first person I could and asked, "Do you know where they do something called looping?"

The person pointed up one of the Paramount streets and said, "Looping Stage L is just beyond Stage Eleven."

This was some added information. Whatever looping is, they do it on a stage. I went up the road and found a door marked "Stage L" and went in. I passed through a couple of sound-proof doors and entered a small engineering studio beyond which was a glass-enclosed recording studio. Ah, new information.

There was a podium, and at the podium was Chris Knight. In front of him was a screen. As soon as I came in, one of the engineers said, "Are you Lloyd?"

"Yes, I am."

"Are you ready?"

"Let's do it."

Then I watched and tried to make sense out of what I was seeing. The screen came to life with the footage from an episode. Wavy black lines preceded three "beeps." Chris listened on headphones and nodded.

The engineer said, "Want to try one?"

Chris said, "Sure."

The footage rolled again, but this time Chris replaced the voice with a new track. Apparently, the sound was wrong for some reason on the original.

The engineer said, "Let's play that back."

The footage rolled, and Chris' new dialogue was inserted. Then it was quiet, and the engineer said to me, "How was that?"

I said the only thing you should say in a situation where you are newly in charge and don't know what's going on: "Not good enough."

"Wow," they all must have thought, "this guy is good." Obviously, I had detected some small flaw they hadn't.

Okay, I bullshitted my way through, but I soon got the hang of looping.

The first episode of Season 2 was a story about Greg becoming a pitcher on his school team. Mike was doing a project with a pro baseball player who comes by the house where he meets Greg and inadvertently gives him the idea that he has a career in the major leagues.

As with several episodes, a little success goes to a Brady kid's head and it leads to big problems. My next problem as production associate was to secure a major league baseball player to be on the show.

I was given a list, and I was pretty excited. I am a huge baseball fan, and my dad had taken me to games ever since the Dodgers had moved to Los Angeles. In fact, when Dad was working on *The Red Skelton Show*, the producer, Cecil Barker, was the first guy to bring a trumpet to the Coliseum where he invented the now-ubiquitous rallying cry, "Charge!"

So which player to call? I called the players representatives and then called the players themselves. Amazing. I got right through. I was actually talking to them. I learned that sports stars are as excited about show business as non athletes are excited about sports stars. Willie Mays was first. Even though he was on the San Francisco Giants (and my natural enemy as a Dodger fan), I owed it to the show to call Willie. I got him on the phone, and I learned he was more nervous talking to me than I was talking to him. I represented a world outside of his comfort zone. Willie Mays was nervous talking to me?! What a world! The same nervousness held true for Dodger Maury Wills who was trying to break into show business. Finally, the decision was made to go with Don Drysdale, also of the Dodgers, and the more logical choice since the episode was about pitching.

I got a glimpse of what it must be like for sports heroes when he came onto the set for filming. One after another of the crew and actors would approach him to recount a favorite game or moment.

I also had my turn at Big D. The difference was that I had hired him so he absolutely had to listen to my memory. This was 1970, and something had been bothering me for 10 years. The moment involved Drysdale, and I finally had the opportunity to clear it up.

"Don, it was 1960. The Dodgers were playing a double-header in the

Coliseum. You weren't pitching in either game. But it was the ninth inning, and the manager decided to use you as a pinch hitter. Anyway, you got up and struck out. You argued, and you were thrown out of the game. I think, since you weren't pitching in either game that day, you did it on purpose. You weren't going to play anyway. Is that why you did it?"

Drysdale thought about it, taking himself back to that day—or so I believed. Then he turned to me and said, "I don't remember the incident."

I was crushed. The one man who could clear it all up "didn't remember the incident." That, and Stonehenge, would have to remain a mystery.

About eight episodes into the new season, I went to Dad again.

"I don't want to appear ungrateful, but I can't see why I can't have the title 'Associate Producer' since that's the job I am doing. The only difference is the salary. Aren't I doing the same as every other associate producer? I think this time you're punishing me because I am your son."

My logic was irrefutable, from my point of view anyway. It was hard for my father since I was a walking symbol of nepotism.

He said, "I needed you to prove yourself—not to me, but to everybody else. And you have."

It was a very Brady Bunch moment, and that is when I became the youngest associate producer in network television. Being "the youngest this" or "the youngest that" is a distinction that everybody has at one time or another, but it doesn't last long.

For me that became very clear when I attended a Paramount screening. In front of me were two executives, and they knew me but didn't know I was sitting behind them. They were discussing a new series with kids that Paramount was putting together. They were considering staffing, and one of them said, "You know the kind of person we need to work with the kids on the show? A young Lloyd Schwartz." I was 23.

Youth is fleeting.

CHAPTER 31

INFLUENCES

Until the episode called "The Slumber Caper" in Season 2, I had little reason to believe we were really having a general impact on our audience. None of my friends were watching, but that made sense. At the time the series was on, I was in my early twenties, exactly the age of the people who wouldn't be watching a family show about parents and their problems with six children.

"The Slumber Caper" had several unusual aspects in the filming itself, and even before filming began. As I explained, our stories had links of plots and subplots. When a plot involved one character, the subplot didn't involve that same character. One simple reason was filming. We couldn't have one child in front of the camera for an entire episode and still enable him or her to finish the required day of schoolwork. In this particular episode, the plot was all about the slumber party Marcia was having, therefore the subplot would necessarily be about the boys. I recalled my junior high days when slumber parties were thrown by the girls. What did teenage boys do? We made life miserable for the girls at the slumber party by playing pranks.

I suggested translating that to the Brady kids. If the girls were having a slumber party, then Greg, Peter, and Bobby would try to disrupt it. There. Plot and subplot all rolled into one.

The shooting gave us the opportunity to make it special for some of the cast members. Both Florence and Robert Reed had daughters Maureen's age. We added Barbara (Florence's daughter) and Karen (Bob Reed's daughter) to the cast of the girls at the slumber party. My own sister, Hope, who had lots of previous acting experience, was to play Jenny, Marcia's friend who was invited, uninvited, then invited again to the party. As an added treat for Bob, we used E.G. Marshall as the school principal. E.G. Marshall and Bob had starred together in *The Defenders*. On the set I was surprised to see that neither seemed to be sentimental about working together again.

Part of the story was taken from a real incident in my father's life. When he was a boy, he had been wrongfully accused of making an ugly drawing of his teacher when he was in school. The truth was that he drew George Washington, but somebody else in a subsequent class in the same room wrote the teacher's name on the drawing. My father is a terrible artist, and apparently the picture was pretty awful looking. He was brought to the principal's office, but he wasn't believed. It must have been pretty traumatic for my father since he remembered it 40 years later. This seemed like a good idea for a show, and we turned the basis of it into the episode.

The show was a good one and was one of the more memorable episodes. However, it made an indelible impression on me because it taught me a lot about the power of TV.

The Brady Bunch was on Friday nights. On the Saturday morning after this episode, I had gone out to breakfast at a local coffee shop. (As a bachelor, I usually went out to breakfast, lunch and dinner.) I was sitting at a table by myself when a large family entered and sat down at the booth adjacent to me.

I overheard the following conversation from two of the boys in the family. Boy Number One said, "Wendy and Francine are having a slumber party tonight."

Boy Number Two said, "Yeah, I know. That won't be any fun for us."

Boy Number One said, "It can be. Remember *The Brady Bunch* last night? The boys messed up the girls' party with itching powder and scary stuff. We can do the same thing."

Boy Number Two said, "That sounds great. Let's do it."

I never introduced myself or told them I had anything to do with the show they had seen, but I was instantly struck by the fact that this was probably not an isolated incident. There were undoubtedly similar conversations happening all around the country. As for our show, we needed a subplot and, because of that, many girls' slumber parties were undoubtedly going to be destroyed by boys imitating our episode.

I have been told by numerous people about the incredible influences *The Brady Bunch* has had on their lives.

One girl told me that she used *The Brady Bunch* as a measuring device to see if she wanted to go out with a guy. Guys who watched the show were date material; guys who didn't, weren't.

One time on a TV news channel in Boston, there was a report that a convict had broken out of a penitentiary and was on the roof. They were trying to talk him down. Finally, to see if the guards were sincere and trustworthy, the escapee said he'd come down if they could name the Brady kids. They did, and he returned to his cell safely.

What is it about prisons and *The Brady Bunch*? I have a friend who told me that he was filming a documentary in a prison and was told the standard garb is the prison uniform and low white tennis shoes that are referred to as "Marcia Bradys" since Marcia often wore that style in our shows.

You just never know.

CHAPTER 32

MARCIA, MARCIA, MARCIA

Dad deliberately didn't want too many topical references in *The Brady Bunch*. He wanted our shows to be universal and not about what was happening currently in the world. That may well be one of the reasons that the shows hold up in syndication.

We have been criticized for not being realistic and not taking on issues of a global nature, but Dad felt that our shows should reflect problems to which all kids and parents could relate, problems that were present in homes of many kinds.

In doing so, we did episodes about peer pressure, acceptance, honesty, etc. Sometimes Dad broke his own rule and did a show that reflected problems that were somewhat topical, and he wanted to address them. Dad showed courage in doing the aforementioned anti-smoking show when there were still cigarette ads on TV.

We also produced a women's lib episode when Marcia wanted to join the all-boy Frontier Scouts and argued sex discrimination. I don't think we used the words "sex discrimination" then because the term had yet to be invented.

Another rule that Dad insisted upon was "no catchphrases." He thought that characters who constantly resorted to expressions like "Sit on it" or "Did I do that?" or "What you talking about, Willis?" would define a show as being part of a specific time and place.

Dad failed. Quite a few expressions have come from *The Brady Bunch*, but few people are aware that each of the Brady catchphrases were only said once in the entire series.

"Mom always said: Don't play ball in the house."

"Pork chops and applesauce."

"Oh, my nose!"

"Something suddenly came up."

"Exact words."

And Dad's and my favorite: "You fit the suit."

Though hardly Shakespearean, many of these lines are quoted as if they were intended to be eternal. And thanks to the show's fans, perhaps they will be.

But by far the most famous quote from a Brady episode is the redundant "Marcia, Marcia, Marcia!" which Jan exclaimed when Marcia's overpowering popularity had gotten just too much for her.

I'm not exactly sure why it has caught on—maybe it's the universality of having that kind of a golden sibling in a family—but "Marcia, Marcia, Marcia" has entered the vernacular and manages to sneak into conversations everywhere.

I apologize to anyone named Marcia or Marsha who can't escape having it as part a cross we have made her bear.

CHAPTER 33

ON THE ROAD

As with any TV series, occasionally the network (and our creative team) thinks that it's a good idea to kick off the new season with a bang. Getting the Brady family out of the house and on the road would be just the right way, so the entire bunch would be off to locations—such as the Grand Canyon.

Both Howard Leeds and Dad had to remain at the studio to prepare future episodes, so I was in charge of the shooting at the Grand Canyon with the director, Oscar Rudolph. In truth, there wasn't much actual shooting at the Grand Canyon. The "ghost town" was actually on the Paramount lot in Hollywood and was where they filmed *Bonanza*. The bottom of the Grand Canyon was in Franklin Canyon in Hollywood. Most of the location shooting involved the tourist stuff on the rim of the Grand Canyon.

Bob Reed had a prior commitment and couldn't do the pre-shoot so he wasn't able to drive the car for the run-bys in front of the Grand Canyon. Who would do it? I was about his height, so the hairstylist dyed my hair black, and I drove the Brady station wagon—though I certainly didn't have his Spiro Agnew-shaped head. Before the dye-job, I was blonde. When my hair grew in, I was suddenly a redhead and stayed that way until most of my hair has receded all the way off my head. I can't scientifically explain my hair turning red. People said that they had never seen that happen before. What we do for our art.

We cheated when we shot the family going to the bottom of the Grand

Canyon on mules. I'm told that the real mule rides to the bottom take a full day. We accomplished our mule ride using dissolves and filming on just the first hundred yards down the trail.

The three-part Grand Canyon episodes kicked off Season 3 of the series. Prior to filming, the six kids did a personal appearance in San Jose, and 120,000 people showed up to see them. I guess people were starting to take notice of the show.

Even so, events can happen which put things in perspective. I was with Florence and the six kids in an elevator at the Bright Angel Lodge at the Grand Canyon. A woman stepped in and saw that she was surrounded by the cast of our situation comedy. She was so knocked out she could hardly speak. After looking at all of us, she turned to Florence and said, "I can't believe it. Shirley, I just love your show. And all you kids, too.

"I just love *The Partridge Family.*" Then she turned to me, mistaking me for Dave Madden. "And Reuben, you're my favorite."

When the elevator door opened, Bob Reed happened to be there and overheard the woman's mistake. He corrected it, saying, "Madam, you were talking about *The Partridge Family*. We are *The Brady Bunch*. They sing; we act."

I think that was the only time I appreciated anything Bob said.

When we were just about to wrap filming, I got a message that I had to go to a party that was ongoing at the Bright Angel Lodge. Several people who had helped arrange for *The Brady Bunch* to shoot in the Grand Canyon were there celebrating our filming. I didn't have time to change since the party was almost ending.

When I arrived in my dust-covered jeans and sweatshirt, I saw a formal party in full swing. Among the attendees were the Governor of Arizona and his wife as well as the Secretary of the Interior and his wife. Also waiting for me were the unit manager, assistant director, and the second assistant director of the series. As it happened, the unit manger was in his seventies and both of his assistants were in their late sixties. As soon as I arrived, Ralph Nelson, the unit manager captured the attention of the party-goers (who apparently had been waiting for me) and provided an introduction.

Ralph said proudly, "Ladies and gentlemen, may I introduce the boss."

I stepped to the front of the room. I had been so busy working I didn't realize how odd this must have looked. I was in my early twenties. These three men who were working for me were over twice as old as I was, and I was "the boss."

I made a short speech thanking them for all they had done in helping our production. In truth, without their cooperation, we wouldn't have been able to film our show there. As I was speaking, I began to notice that much of the audience was open-mouthed. In their businesses, people who were in charge were the ones with the most experience. When I finished, the wife of the Governor of Arizona raised her hand.

"May I ask a question?"

"Sure."

"You look so young."

Now I realized why everybody seemed surprised when I was addressing them.

"To explain," I said, "the producers are back in Hollywood getting the other episodes ready, and I am in charge here representing them. And I am young. What can I say? Everybody is young once."

They laughed.

"Thank you again," I said.

We were lucky to have Jay Silverheels as a guest star. As Tonto on *The Lone Ranger*, he was always one of my favorite actors. For some reason, I have always liked the sidekick better than the heroes.

Just as with Don Drysdale, I had the opportunity to clear up something that had always bothered me.

I asked him, "When you played Tonto, you had the greatest 'hmmmmm.' And 'hmmmmm, Kemo Sabe.' It was so wise. Could you tell me what that looked like in the script? Was it 'hmmmm,' or 'mmmmm'? Or something else?"

He said, "It was never in the script at all. They would usually have a line that I thought was stupid, so I just replaced it with 'hmmmm.'"

I got an answer, but it certainly wasn't the one I expected.

Another example of impact came from Tam Spiva who had been a college friend of Bob Reed's at Northwestern. Tam Spiva was our story editor, and he was the writer of the three-part Grand Canyon episodes. At the end of the second part, Bobby and Cindy were lost in the wilds of the canyon, and the Brady family has spread out to look for them. Each of them called for the missing children: "Bobby! Cindy! Bobby! Cindy!" And on their desperation the episode faded out. Tam reported that after the episode, his own young children decided to aid in the search by going around their house yelling, "Bobby! Cindy! Bobby! Cindy!" He said the constant hollering of "Bobby! Cindy!" in Tam's house didn't stop until the two youngest Brady kids were found a week later in Part Three.

As with the slumber party episode, I'm sure other families had children screaming for a week, and I apologize.

CHAPTER 34

HUMPHREY WHO?

It was the early 1970s and cable television wasn't widely available yet; neither were VCRs. There were few places that people could go to watch old movies. Therefore it was logical that Chris Knight had never heard of Humphrey Bogart.

Chris got the script for the episode "The Personality Kid," which was all about him being told he was dull and trying to find a new personality for himself. He tries borrowing other people's personalities, and one of them was Humphrey Bogart's. When the script said he asks Alice what she is serving for dinner, she tells him, "Pork chops and applesauce."

According to the script he is supposed to respond (a la Humphrey Bogart), "Pork chops and applesauce, huh? That's swell."

Never having heard of Bogey, he didn't know how to play it. There were no Blockbuster video rentals. There were no videos at all, let alone DVDs. It would be a matter of waiting for a Bogart movie to come on some channel somewhere or finding a print and arranging a screening. Fortunately, it was not supposed to be a good impression anyway. In truth, Chris had the worst ear of any one of the kids. When they sang, he was usually asked to just mouth the words.

One time, in one of the very first episodes, he was supposed to say, "Aren't *you* going with us?" The pronoun "you" was supposed to be stressed like "Aren't *you* going with us?"

Chris would say, "*Aren't* you going with us?"

As dialogue coach I would repeat to him, "Say it this way: Aren't *you* going with us?"

He listened to me, tried his best, and it would still come out: "*Aren't* you going with us?"

That went on for five or six more times, but he never got it. It's buried in one of the early episodes, and it was never right.

So the chances of Chris watching Bogart and doing an accurate impression weren't very good.

He asked, "Who exactly is Humphrey Bogart?"

"It doesn't matter, Chris," I said. "Just do it like this. . . ."

At which point I did my very best Humphrey Bogart impression, which wasn't all that good either.

"Pork chops and apple sauce, huh? Isn't that swell?"

Chris did the scene and, to this day, he still has people coming up to him on a regular basis asking him: "Say it. Come on, say it."

He politely obliges: "Pork chops and applesauce, huh? Isn't that swell?"

But when they ask him about his impression of Humphrey Bogart, he always corrects them. He says, "I never did a Humphrey Bogart impression. I just did an impression of Lloyd Schwartz doing an impression of Humphrey Bogart."

CHAPTER 35

AT THE MARKET

The episode "And Now a Word from Our Sponsor"—a fan favorite in which the Bradys almost starred in a TV commercial but were fired thanks to bad acting advice from a ditzy ex-actress—was actually a traumatic episode to shoot on several fronts.

First, it brought forth another diatribe from Robert Reed who was terribly upset about the reality of a typical American family doing a TV commercial. He didn't like the performance of Paul Winchell, who played the commercial director Skip Farnum. He didn't like the endorsement of a product by a family. He didn't like . . . actually, he didn't like anything about it. If we listened to Robert, episodes would be nothing more than him lecturing.

Far more traumatic was the actual filming at the supermarket where the Brady family is first discovered by Skip Farnum for the commercial.

As associate producer, I went with the director of the episode, Peter Baldwin, to the market the day before to set the opening shot. Opening shots are usually wide shots that require the most lighting and the most set-up time. You do those first so that the crew has the most time to prepare for them in anticipation of the cast's arrival.

I got to the set about 6:30 on the morning of shooting, and I noticed immediately that the camera was not where we had placed it the day before. I went over to Peter, who wasn't his normally exuberant self.

"What's up? I thought the camera was supposed to be over there."

Peter just pointed to the place in the parking lot where we had placed the camera position the previous day.

I went over to that spot and was shocked to see a dead body with a blanket over his head. His heavy work shoes were sticking out. I crossed to the studio guard who was waving a red flag to stop traffic from entering the market.

"Do you know what happened?

This guard knew far too well.

"He had a heart attack."

"Gee, that's too bad."

He waved the flag mournfully when he added, "And he was my best friend."

Indeed, the body was that of another studio guard who had been working as a watchman for studio equipment, and who had died at his post.

"I'm so sorry."

The guard kept waving his flag as I went back to Peter.

Peter said, "We can get an establishing shot of the market from here and maybe get some other things while we wait for the coroner to take the body away."

That's what we did. Shooting went as smoothly as it could under the circumstances, and then I walked over to see our unit manager, Ralph Nelson, who was re-adjusting the shooting schedule to see what we could shoot next without the cast. There wasn't anything. He turned to the assistant director.

"Notify the studio to send in the kids."

I quickly looked over to where the guard's body was still lying. I turned to the assistant director and countermanded the unit manager's orders.

"Don't send in the kids."

It was a stand-off. The unit manager was annoyed with me. He had to finish the show, and I was making the show fall behind.

"We need the cast, or we can't shoot anything."

"I know, but we're not going to have the kids here while a dead man is lying there. We're going to wait for the coroner to arrive to take away the body."

Ralph looked at his paperwork and report. His job was to get the show done on time come hell or high water—or corpses.

"How can I explain this in my report?"

I told him to open to the page of his production report where he was to write down the reasons for any unnatural delays.

"Put down: 'Associate producer unreasonable.' And if anyone asks why, I'll be happy to explain it."

He wrote down what I asked him to. No one asked anything since we finished the day on time.

Also at the filming in the market, I began a long-lasting relationship with John Lenox, a young man who was destined to become my best friend and business partner. At that time, John was a second assistant trainee, and his job was to direct background action.

In TV shows and movies, while the actors are directed by the director, the people who cross in the background are directed by an assistant director whose job is to make sure that everything looks natural. The audience should be unaware that this is happening, and it should all look as if the actors are acting in the real world and not in a void.

John was sending extras through at an appropriate pace and making sure that their activities weren't obtrusive.

Later, when I looked at the film I noticed that he had a small scene going on in the background. It wasn't distracting from the scene with the actors and it looked natural, but it was more than the traditional crosses back and forth that most assistant directors arrange.

I studied the background action. A man and a woman meet. The man takes out his wallet. The woman shakes her head as if they were haggling over a price. Finally, she nods her head, and then they walk off together. In the background of a *Brady Bunch* episode, John subversively had staged a scene of a prostitute picking up a client.

Nobody else noticed this activity. You'd have to pay strict attention to even see it, but I knew that anybody who had this quirky sense of humor and could pull this off was someone I had to get to know better. John went on to produce many shows and movies. We produced many things together, and he was godfather to my son, Andrew. We remained close friends until he died far too prematurely on his fiftieth birthday. I'll miss him forever.

CHAPTER 36

FOR A SONG

The Brady Bunch was not a series about a singing group of kids. That was *The Partridge Family*. There was a perceived rivalry and sometimes a confusion between the two shows. In truth, they were easy to differentiate from one another. *The Partridge Family* was a series based on the Cowsills, a popular family singing group, and each week Shirley Jones, David Cassidy, et al, would weave a song into their episodes.

The distinction grew cloudy when the Brady kids would sing in certain episodes. Maybe the kids sang in seven out of the 117 episodes. And in two or three, Florence did. Some of the Brady songs have had continued success which makes people believe our six kids sang more than they did.

All of our singing episodes were plot driven; usually the Brady kids had to try to figure out what to do to raise some extra money. They would get together to enter a singing contest of some kind, and there'd be a problem.

One of the problems featured came directly from the inability of Chris Knight to carry a tune in real life. That would later become a problem for the other kids when they wanted to sing as a group, and Peter was tone deaf. In the episode about his voice changing, Chris was so tone deaf he couldn't even sing the note which was supposed to show him being tone deaf. Our producer, Howard Leeds, hit that note. Howard had a deep voice, and it didn't quite sound like Chris—but it sure made the point.

And that wasn't the only time Howard—or at least a part of him—appeared in the series. In the episode where Greg made a home movie about the pilgrims, "The Un-underground Movie," Howard drenched his own foot with water as the pilgrim who landed on Plymouth Rock.

Now back to the music. In another episode, Monkees lead singer Davy Jones was a guest star. At the time, the Monkees were a hot group, so Davy's appearance was a much bigger deal to our cast of children than it was to him. He was much in demand and had a certain above-it-all star attitude. A few years ago I ran into Davy, who reported that his being on *The Brady Bunch* was something he always gets asked about, and he has to sing the song he sang on our show whenever he does his act.

Florence was and is a great singer. She sang a Christmas song in one of the first episodes. Later, she and Maureen did a duet in a parent/child talent show and sang "Together" from *Gypsy*. Maureen didn't even realize how much of a challenge it was to sing with a genuine Broadway musical star and, because of that, did it easily.

Talent shows, amateur contests, etc. gave the Brady family their reasons for singing. We were blessed that Barry, Maureen, and Mike were very musical. Eve and Susan were okay, and then there was poor Chris, who really didn't like singing at all.

We filmed our series from June to December. After shooting ended for the year, Dad wanted the kids to recapture as much of their lives as possible by returning to their own schools. He thought that it would be better for them, and that's what we thought they were doing. But much to our surprise, they weren't. I don't know how or when it all started, but some of the parents—or an agent or manager—thought that there was money to be made if the kids actually became a singing group and went on the road.

When we found out about it, Dad could have stopped it or at least he could have taken a share of the money since the six kids didn't have the legal right or permission to call themselves *The Brady Bunch*, or *The Brady Kids*. But he thought if they wanted to make some money, it was not right for him to stand in their way.

They were keeping all of this a secret from us, and for good reason. Kids are only supposed to work on a show for a limited number of hours. That is to protect them. But there were no laws about doing work after leaving the set. After filming our show for the day, they would go off to rehearse for hours. There were no welfare rules off the set. They would come in tired for filming the next day, and I didn't know why.

The first time I found out anything about it was when I got them all together to re-sing the theme song for the third season. They balked and wanted it to be much more professional. I wanted it as before; I wanted them to sound like kids singing it like a camp song. They wanted harmonies and perfect pitch.

"After all," said Barry, "We're a singing group."

Then they all told me what they have been doing. Their parents had been setting up a tour for their children as a musical group. When a series is successful, the smell of money wafts in. Though we remained close for a long time, we all realized that not all of us had the same vision. What was it that Oscar Rudolph said about "Never trust an actor"?

For a year or two, they performed a lot. One of their biggest gigs was on the Steel Pier in Atlantic City. We really didn't know anything about their tour or exactly where they were playing, but they toured nationally. Later on, they were on a special of *The Ed Sullivan Show* from Las Vegas, and Dad and I and some of the other Schwartzes went to see them. This was the first time I realized what their act was really about. It was a bit of a shock.

By the time they finished as a singing group, they recorded a few albums. And recently, Brady music has become a symbol of the 60s, and the song "Sunshine Day" is a retro-hit.

CHAPTER 37

BOYS MEET GIRLS

An unspoken responsibility that became part of my job was hormone patrol. The Brady kids were attractive to America—and attractive to each other. Each of them had an opposite-sex counterpart with whom they were spending an inordinate amount of time. It is only natural that relationships would begin to develop.

Much has been written and exaggerated about the nonexistent affair between Barry and Florence. Florence was happily married with four kids. Barry was happily horny with unrealistic aspirations. Barry was very interested in music, and Florence was an expert. He asked her to go along with him to see a singer at a concert or club. They went. I'm not sure who drove, but she politely kissed him good-night—on the cheek, from what I understand. This is the extent of the "affair" between Barry and Florence. Sorry, I wish I could make that more salacious, but it wasn't.

The real issues that were developing were the crushes that Barry had on Maureen and Maureen had on Barry. Fortunately, much of the time they alternated on who liked who. They never seemed to be of a similar mind at the same time. Barry complicated Maureen's interest in him by having a parade of girlfriends. At the beginning of the show, Maureen wasn't ready for boys. That lasted about a year.

All I knew was that passion was imminent, and that it would be destructive.

On-set relationships between adult stars are tricky—not so much when the relationship is going well, but when dating stars break up and they have to continue acting with each other, all hell breaks loose. If it's complicated for adults who have had relationships before, for teen-agers (who have no prior experiences) it's even more difficult.

It would be simpler if they just didn't start anything. Noticing increased eye contact and giggling between Barry and Maureen, I decided to go into a preventative strategy. I took Barry aside and appealed to his vanity.

"Barry, I want to talk to you about Maureen."

"Sure. What?"

"She's cute. Really cute. And you know the best thing about really cute girls? They have really cute friends. You're a good-looking guy. You can use Maureen to meet some of her cute girlfriends. That way you'll always have a large field of girls."

As an afterthought I added, "And besides, if you get something going with Maureen, it could only limit you."

I think Barry bought the logic.

Chris and Eve were eyeing each other as well. They had couple potential, but at that age, girls develop faster than boys, and Chris was oblivious about Eve's advanced interest. After the series, Chris and Eve went out. I've had no reports.

As for Mike and Susan, it was mutual puppy love. They were then, and are now, good friends.

Along with my script, I carried a metaphorical bucket of water to try to cool down libidos.

After the second season, I got a request from Paramount and ABC. Barry was becoming a teen idol, and they thought a promotional trip would help create more interest in him, and in the show. I was asked to take him on a publicity tour as a guardian.

We traveled around the country and made stops at various TV and radio stations for interviews. It was interesting for me since I hadn't done anything like that before. Our first stop was the "I Am an American Day Parade" in Baltimore.

The parade drew 750,000 spectators with 33,000 in the parade. We rode in a convertible with Barry sitting on the rear seat and waving at fans. My job was more intense. I rode in the front and prevented teenage-girl fans from swarming Barry under. I literally had to knock them off of the car.

After Baltimore we flew to other cities. Barry was recognized wherever we went. On one of the legs of the trip, we started talking to some attractive flight attendants who weren't bothered by how young he was. I was impressed with how he was holding his own. They suggested we all go back to the hotel.

Barry kept wondering how we were going to get the girls to separate. I wasn't worried, but this was a new experience for him. Finally, I said, "See you in the morning, Barry," and shoved him to his room with one of the fight attendants.

The next morning, Barry staggered into my room after the girls had left. His eyes were as big as Frisbees. I guess that's where the expression, "He really had his eyes opened," comes from.

The trip was also beneficial regarding the burgeoning relationship between Barry and Maureen. It elevated him way past Maureen as far as experience.

Recently, Barry and I were working on a play together and I asked him about his book.

"How come you didn't write about the stewardesses on our trip around the country while *The Brady Bunch* was on the air? That would have made some pretty good reading in your book."

Barry said, "I thought about it, but it didn't make me look that good."

CHAPTER 38

ALOHA

The Hawaii episodes that started Season 4 are among the most remembered by the fans—and the cast. We hired a director, Jack Arnold, who was used to shooting on location and used to finishing fast, which was helpful since there is only so much daylight. It also gave the cast and crew the chance to enjoy all that Hawaii has to offer.

I made an error in Hawaii which almost destroyed the hard work I had put in keeping the kids off of one another. I met an attractive woman who was working at our hotel. Hawaii inspires romance, and I thought I'd take her on a moonlit walk along the beach. I confess I used the fact that I was a producer of *The Brady Bunch* to make me seem more intriguing. I thought it would be fun to have the Brady kids walk along with us. Big error. The moon, the night, the stars, the beach, the waves—oops. We barely all made it back before they were on top of each other. It took me weeks to undo my mistake.

One of the first scenes we filmed was the Brady family arriving at the hotel. Sounds like a simple shot, right? Not so. Anytime a show films on location, crowd control becomes an issue. Hawaii is all tourists, and all tourists at the hotel became a crowd that wanted to see their favorite TV family. By the time we got the shot lined up, there were 500 people (no exaggeration) all crammed onto the sidewalk—and all in our shot. The Brady family is supposed to be an average American family, so 500 spectators would not normally be cheering upon their entrance to the hotel. What to do? I grabbed the bullhorn and told the crowd:

"We want you all to be in our show. So here is what I need you to do. When I yell 'Action!' follow me over this way. And don't look at the camera, or we can't use the shot."

They were thrilled. They thought they were going to be on TV. What I didn't tell them was that the camera was not going to be following them. As soon as I got them out of the camera line, the camera would then start rolling and pan away from the tourists to capture the Brady vehicle arrive, seemingly alone, as they went into the hotel.

My deception worked. I felt bad, but not nearly as badly as I would have felt if I had 500 unexplained people yelling at the Brady bunch: "Marcia, I love you!" "Florence, I have all your albums!" etc.

Some things reach the level of legend and don't belong there at all. Much has been written about how *The Brady Bunch* actors almost died in a horrible accident on an outrigger canoe in the waves off of Waikiki. Sorry. It never happened. I have even read different accounts of the harrowing ordeal where Florence saved Susan from certain death, or Barry saved Mike, or Chris saved Eve. No one really saved anybody.

We were filming the family in an outrigger canoe. I was with the crew in another outrigger alongside. The boats got too close together. Our boat nudged their boat. There was a little wobbling. The crew got out of our canoe and held the camera equipment over their heads so as not to land in the water. We walked to shore. It was that shallow. The tale has been blown out of proportion so as to rival the sinking of the *Titanic*.

Barry was very athletic in real life. In the show we filmed Greg having a surfing accident. For the filming Barry didn't want a stunt man since he was a good surfer. In contrast to the non-dramatic outrigger incident, Barry's surfing wipe-out was more dangerous than it appeared. In Hawaii, the coral heads lie close to the surface and can do some real damage. Barry fell off of his board for real and scraped himself on the coral heads. Fortunately, he was okay, but it was close.

The overall shooting went well, and on the night before the last day of filming there was a party for the cast and crew. I'm not much of a drinker, and Hawaii is well-known for its abundance of rum drinks. I had something called a Zombie. From its name I should have known not to have more than one, or in my case, *half* of one. I was into my second or third—I can't remember now, and I couldn't remember then—when I guess I asked Florence to dance.

Florence is a great dancer. I'm not. She is the kind of dancer who makes her dancing partner think he's a great dancer because she happily follows all of his inept moves. Anyway, while I was dancing with Florence, the drink took over, and I don't remember anything more about the evening. No, I didn't go home with her. I certainly would have remembered that.

The next day, Florence took me aside.

"If I ever told your father what you asked me to do. . . ."

She left it at that. I don't remember saying anything, but I guess I did make some sort of immodest proposal.

The story doesn't end there. Florence and I now have the same doctor. Every six months or so, he calls me up.

"Lloyd, this is David."

"Oh, hi, David. What's up?"

"Guess who I have in my office."

"Florence?"

"That's right."

"Is she naked?"

"Not yet."

"Call me back when she is."

At that point—and this happens every six months—Florence yells to David so that I can hear: "Ask him about Hawaii!"

Now, you see why everybody loves Florence.

Lloyd when he was sitting down, which was rare.

Mike, the budding cameraman.

Mike and Susan riding in a parade.
(The Bradys rode in a lot of parades.)

One of the millions of Brady fans
who showed up at malls, parades, and other
events to see their favorite stars in person.

Susan and Mike petting a new furry friend.

Some of the Brady kids feeding a baby elephant.

Maureen, Ann B., Mike and
Susan with a baby chimp.

Susan and her mother, Dee, in Hawaii.

Sherwood during the Hawaii episodes.

Mike at the Arizona Memorial in Hawaii.

(left to right) Sam Kapua and Don Ho with Susan and Mike.

(left to right) Crew members, Chris, Vincent Price, Mike, Barry and Lloyd in the cave from the Hawaii episodes.

Publicity from the Hawaii episodes.

A contemplative Mike.

A smiling Maureen.

Lloyd—in his 1970s pants—and Susan.

Robert (commenting on the script) and Florence (in Mrs. Brady's most popular hairdo).

Brady kids dressed in period costumes from the Jesse James dream sequence.

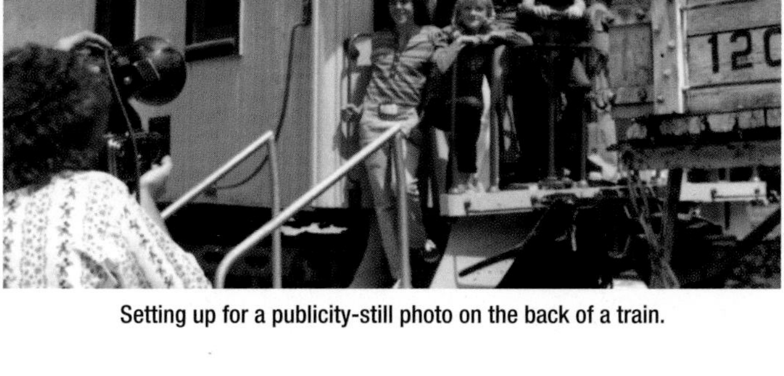

Setting up for a publicity-still photo on the back of a train.

The girls and their parents in the girls' bedroom. Looks like someone is about to learn a lesson. . . .

Lloyd showing Joe Namath how to throw a pass.

A publicity still from one of the middle seasons.

Sherwood, Barry, and Nelson Rockefeller.

The Brady kids with Henry Kissinger and his family.

The Bradys meet the Partridges.

Roy Rogers meets some Bradys on the set.

Mildred Schwartz, Mike, and Mrs. Whitfield.

Celebrating our 100th episode. Who knew we would go this long?

Lloyd at King's Island.

Maureen and Eve at King's Island.

(left to right) Ann B.'s twin sister Harriet, Howard Leeds, Ann B., Dee Olsen, "the Sooz," and Lloyd at King's Island.

Bob Reed sporting his own mid-’70s look.

Florence in her own hairdo in the mid ’70s.

The Brady Bunch cast, with Sherwood in the middle, in one of the later seasons.

Lots of novelty items—like this Brady Bunch lunchbox—were made at the peak of the series' popularity.

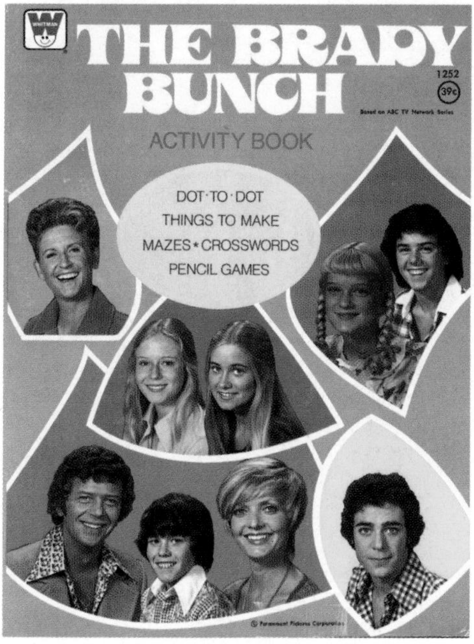

With great popularity comes great literature—
or at least, novelty books.

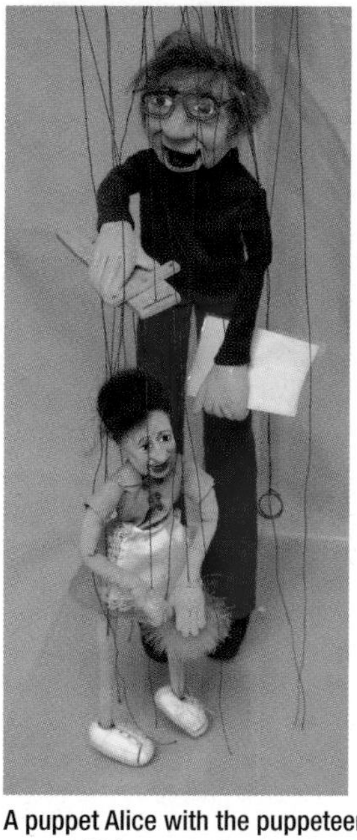

A puppet Alice with the puppeteer Sherwood. This was a cherished present from Ann B. Davis to Sherwood.

Mike with our regular stand-ins, Frankie and Sadie Delfino.

Stand-ins Frankie and Sadie Delfino in their first and only appearance on the show as actors when they guest-starred as "Kaplutians"—with Sherwood, Astronaut James McDivitt, Florence and Susan.

Florence, Sherwood, Astronaut James McDivitt, Ann B. and Robert on the set of the "Out of This World" episode.

The Brady kids' fathers behind each of the kids, with Sherwood. (left to right) Neely Plumb, Ed Knight, Richard McCormick, Frank Blenkhorn, Larry Olsen, and Paul Lookinland.

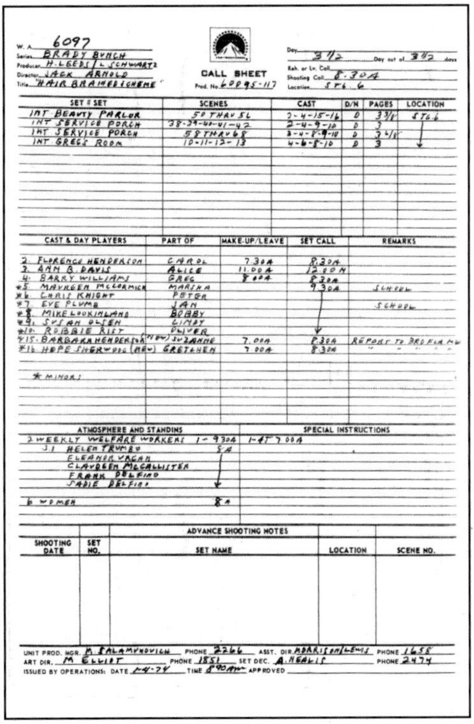

W. A. 6097
Series BRADY BUNCH
Producer H. LEEDS / L. SCHWARTZ
Director JACK ARNOLD
Title "HAIR BRAINED SCHEME"

CALL SHEET
Prod. No. 60095-117

Day 3 1/2 Day out of 3 1/2 days
Reh. or Lv. Call
Shooting Call 8.30A
Location STG. 6

SET # SET	SCENES	CAST	D/N	PAGES	LOCATION
INT BEAUTY PARLOR	50 THRU 56	2-4-15-16	D	3 3/8	STG 6
INT SERVICE PORCH	38-39-40-41-42	2-4-9-10	D	3	↓
INT SERVICE PORCH	58 THRU 68	2-4-8-9-10	D	3 6/8	
INT GREGS ROOM	10-11-12-13	4-6-8-10	D	3	

CAST & DAY PLAYERS	PART OF	MAKE-UP/LEAVE	SET CALL	REMARKS
2. FLORENCE HENDERSON	CAROL	7.30A	8.30A	
3. ANN B. DAVIS	ALICE	11.00A	12.00N	
4. BARRY WILLIAMS	GREG	8.00A	8.30A	
*5. MAUREEN McCORMICK	MARSHA		9.30A	SCHOOL
*6. CHRIS KNIGHT	PETER			
*7. EVE PLUMB	JAN			SCHOOL
*8. MIKE LOOKINLAND	BOBBY			
*9. SUSAN OLSEN	CINDY			
*10. ROBBIE RIST	OLIVER		↓	
*15. BARBARA HENDERSON (NEW)	SUZANNE	7.00A	8.30A	REPORT TO 3RD FLR MW
*16. HOPE SHERWOOD (NEW)	GRETCHEN	7.00A	8.30A	" " " "
* MINORS				

ATMOSPHERE AND STANDINS	SPECIAL INSTRUCTIONS
2 WEEKLY WELFARE WORKERS 1 - 9.30A	1-AT 7.00A
S.I. HELEN TRUMBO 8A	
ELEANOR VAGAN	
CLAUDEEN McCALLISTER	
FRANK DELFINO	
SADIE DELFINO ↓	
6 WOMEN 8A	

ADVANCE SHOOTING NOTES

SHOOTING DATE	SET NO.	SET NAME	LOCATION	SCENE NO.

UNIT PROD. MGR. M. SALAMUNOVICH PHONE 2266 ASST. DIR. MORRISON/LEWIS PHONE 1658
ART DIR. M. ELLIOT PHONE 1851 SET DEC. A. NEALIS PHONE 2474
ISSUED BY OPERATIONS: DATE 1-4-74 TIME 8.40 AM APPROVED

The original series' last-episode call sheet.

On the stairs for *The Brady Girls Get Married*.

The cast of *The Brady Brides*. (top to bottom) Ron Kuhlman, Eve Plumb, Jerry Houser, and Maureen McCormick.

Robert and Sherwood *still* discussing/arguing.

The Brady Bunch in the White House cast, with Lloyd in the middle.

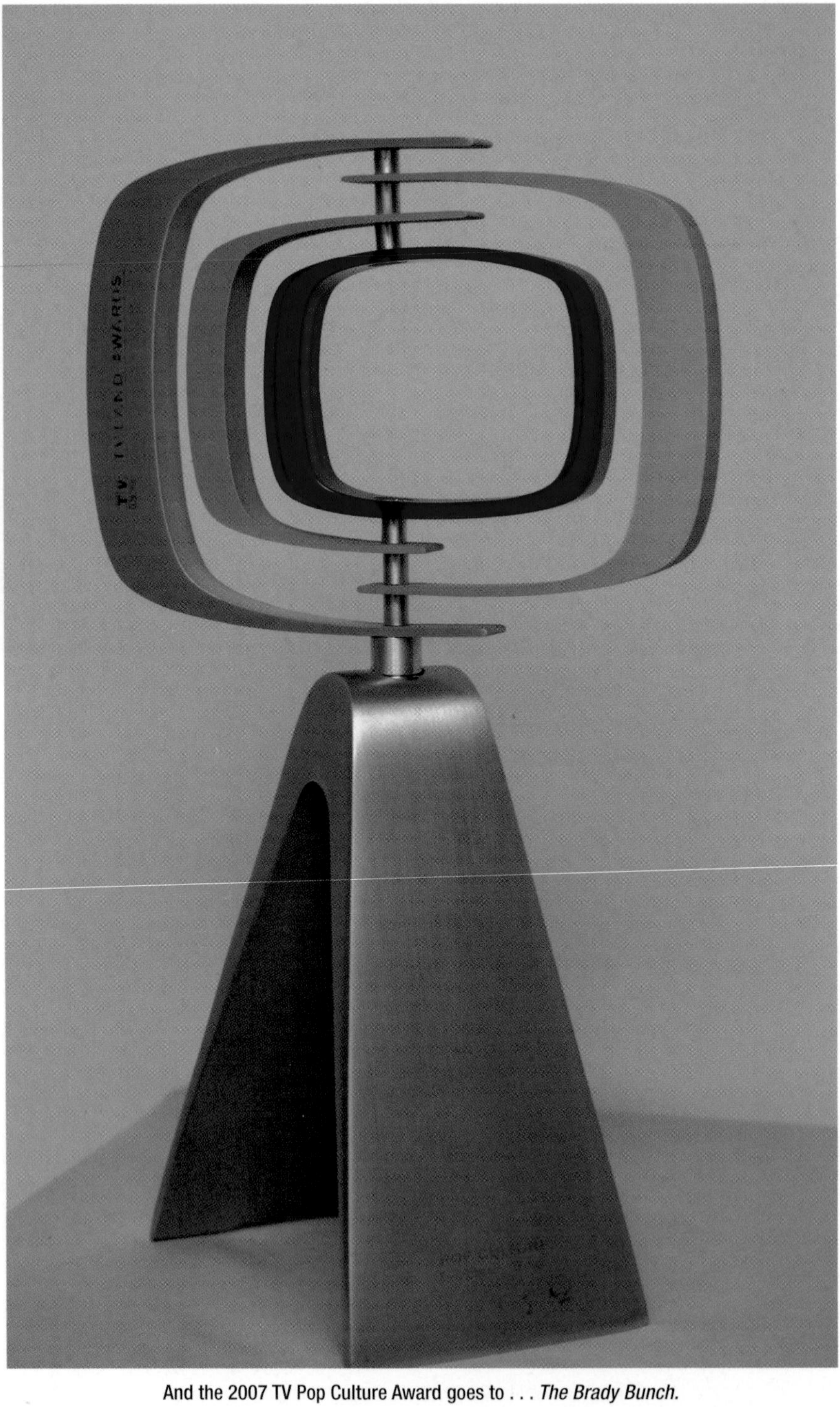

And the 2007 TV Pop Culture Award goes to . . . *The Brady Bunch.*

CHAPTER 39

SOME NAME THINGS

I was watching *Who Wants to Be a Millionaire?* recently and one of the last questions was about *The Brady Bunch.* Since our series has gone off the air, there have always been references on game shows, let alone on regular TV shows and movies. *Jeopardy!* has had entire categories about *The Brady Bunch.*

In *Who Wants to Be a Millionaire?* the question was about Carol Brady's maiden name. I believe the choices were Nelson, Franklin, Martin, and Tyler. The answer? Tyler. Martin was Carol's married name by her first husband. I think the contestant got it right.

The people who worked on *Who Wants to Be a Millionaire?* were obviously Brady fans because the names were relevant to the show. Nelson is Alice's surname, and Alice became Alice Franklin when she finally married Sam between the show's cancellation and the premiere of *A Very Brady Christmas.*

Dad never had given a last name to Alice in the beginning of the series. In the presentation, Alice was just Alice. Alice got her last name when we were filming an episode in which a mailman came to the door and said he had a letter for Alice. The actor, John Wheeler, looked at me and said, "What's Alice's last name? I can't just have a letter for 'Alice.'"

He was right. No one knew. I said, "Nelson."

In the scene, he said, "I have a letter for Alice Nelson."

I picked Nelson in a salute to *Ozzie and Harriet* since Dad worked on that show when it was on the radio.

In another episode, we were filming in Sam's Butcher Shop and Sam had to give someone his last name. Alan Melvin, who played Sam, asked me what his last name was. I said "Franklin" for no particular reason other than Ben Franklin is on the $100 bill and there was a money transaction in the scene.

Nelson and Franklin were two of the choices for the contestant on *Who Wants to Be a Millionaire?* and it's lucky he chose neither—though few people knew how they got to be two of the names the contestant had to choose from.

Here's a bit of trivia. The name of the street where the fictional Brady family live is Clinton Avenue, the name of a real street in Los Angeles. The name "Clinton" had nothing to do with Bill or Hillary Clinton. Remember we were on long before Bill Clinton came to office. I suggested "Clinton" to Dad since it was the name of the street where his parents lived for many years.

In every series and in many movies, characters need names, and on *The Brady Bunch* we often tried to have fun with it by naming characters after people we knew. Jerry Rogers was a quarterback in one episode, and he was named after our assistant editor. Hank Coleman had a crush on Jan or Marcia, and the real Hank Coleman was a vice-president of Paramount Studios—he took the script page that had "Hank Coleman" on it and framed it on his office wall. The Pete Sterne Amateur Hour was named after our representative from ABC. While I was the dialogue coach, I had to smile when Lloyd's Stereo City was named after me. A dentist was named Stanley Vogel after Howard Leed's real dentist. An astronaut was named Dick Whitfield after Frances Whitfield's husband. For years I would ask Frances about her modest husband by saying, "How's the astronaut?"

Many movies and TV shows do the same thing. I became an executive at ABC after *The Brady Bunch* went off the air, and in some kind of odd tribute to me, several shows got together and all named characters "Lloyd" one week. Sounds like an honor? Maybe not since all those characters named "Lloyd" were in dramatic shows and were bigamists, rapists and bank robbers. I choose not to consider what they must have thought about me.

Beside my sister, who is a talented actress, we were lucky to have other people who were actors within the Brady family. We used them in roles on the shows. Chris Knight's father, Ed, played the host of a game show. Todd Lookinland, Mike's brother, was one of *The Kelly Kids*, a show that we intended to spin off from *The Brady Bunch.*

We were able to give many actors their starts on the series as well. Marcia Wallace (the secretary on *The Bob Newhart Show*) did one of her first TV appearances on the show, as did Marion Ross (Richie Cunningham's mother on *Happy Days*) and Gordon Jump (the boss on *WKRP in Cincinatti*).

Rita Wilson got her Screen Actor's Guild card for a role on *The Brady Bunch* and later became Tom Hanks' wife.

We had first-time writers and directors, too, who got their start on our show. Feature film director Alan Rudolph was an assistant director on the show, and film director Gregory Hoblit was a dialogue coach.

I'm proud to say that on a Saturday morning show, *Big John, Little John*, I gave a first writing assignment to Jim Abrahams, Jerry Zucker, and David Zucker who went on to write and direct *Airplane* and a whole string of box office smashes (together and separately) like *Naked Gun*, *Ghost*, etc.

And I'm equally proud of Peter Casey (creator of *Frasier*, etc.) whose career I launched as a dialogue coach on one of the *Gilligan* TV movies.

The important thing to remember about giving people their start is to make sure they are talented. Giving friends or relatives jobs only hurts everyone if they can't deliver. We made sure everyone was qualified who broke in on our shows.

As for me, Dad has always been proudest of my accomplishments that were achieved from jobs that were given me from people who met me on the series and then asked me to work with them away from *The Brady Bunch*.

CHAPTER 40

BLOWING UP

The plot was a true Brady kind of plot. Marcia wants to be popular so she joins a snooty girls club at the high school.

Now we had to think of a subplot. By the third year of the show, we had it down to a science. Our formula—one child at the center of the show, and another child (or the parents or Alice) at the center of the subplot—was clicking along. By this time, we had discovered that adult stories as the main plots had a tendency to leave the kids out of the action, so we always tried to make both plot and subplot about the kids. If you look back at the episodes you'll see the vast majority of them were about the kids.

What would this particular subplot be? I always prided myself on finding solutions quickly, but I was stumped. We were all stumped. Dad, Howard Leeds, script editor Skip Webster, and I were sitting in Dad's office and looking at each other. I was getting more and more upset that I couldn't think of anything. I felt like I was going to explode. Dad saw my angst and said, "What's the matter?"

"I feel like I'm going to explode!"

"What do you mean 'explode'?"

Just like that, it all came to me in a burst.

"Explode. Like a volcano explodes. Peter is building a volcano for a science project at school. That runs through the episode while Marcia is deciding to join the club. She finally is selected to join the club, but when the girls from the club are all over at the Brady house, the volcano explodes—all over the snooty girls."

Dad said, "I like it."

That's how the episode came to be; all because I was upset that I couldn't think of anything.

Just as with many episodes, I drew from life experience. I had been fascinated with volcanoes, actually all kind of disasters. I am drawn to stories about floods, earthquakes, tidal waves, etc.

In junior high I had made a small guillotine for history class and also built a *papier mache* volcano.

I met with the special effects people about the volcano that Peter would build. The one I built in my junior high class was a pretty sorry one. Peter's wasn't. And his exploded right on cue, thanks to the wizardry of the Paramount special effects department.

As a rule, associate producers don't receive much fan mail. Stars and the show itself get lots of letters from fans. On this episode, however, I got several letters from kids who wanted to build a working volcano for their science fairs. They asked how we did it. I didn't really know, so I wrote them that it was trickier than it looked. "But if you want to build one just like the one we had on our show, first, get two special effects men. . . ."

This episode was a prime example of the moral spine of *The Brady Bunch*. Whoever does something wrong, gets it in the end. In this case, the snooty girls get covered in mud. The series always followed that rule, so if one of the kids gets a big head or tries to find a way around a rule, he or she pays the consequences. Apparently, Paramount found additional value in this perspective. Oxford Films—a division of Paramount Television—edited selected *Brady* episodes down to seven or eight minutes and made them available to schools as educational films.

CHAPTER 41

JESSE JAMES

Even though we never had any censorship issues regarding any of the words or images in our shows, one time we got a call from the network about one of our storylines. When the show was airing, there was a rash of airplane hijackings. This was before the tragedy of terrorist hijackings, but at the time people would take over planes for other reasons. Sometimes, they were seeking asylum in other countries. One famous high-jacking was by a man named D.B. Cooper who had taken over a plane for money and supposedly jumped out safely, never to be found again.

Some kids thought these modern-day highwaymen were heroes, and we thought it would be a good idea for a story if Bobby idolized one of these people and wrote a school paper about him as someone he admired.

We were excited about the story and were extremely disappointed when our story was turned down by the network. They explained their point of view. The story was constructed in a way that Bobby would spend a significant amount of time building up the skyjacker and extolling how brave he was until Bobby learned how the skyjacker endangered people.

For the majority of the half-hour show, the children in our audience would think that Bobby was right—until he learned his lesson later. What if they tuned out the show before it ended? They'd be left with the wrong message.

We listened to the network and reluctantly had to agree with them. We felt responsible to our audience and certainly didn't want to influence children negatively, even though at the end of the episode Bobby learned that people like skyjackers were not to be admired.

However, we didn't want to give up on the theme: Admire people worthy of admiration, not people who do exciting things that bring harm to other people.

We thought about it, and Dad came up with the idea of switching the story to someone from the past. What if Bobby admired Jesse James? Our audience couldn't be influenced to become old Western outlaws.

The show was rewritten in that way. And, though it may not be anybody else's, it's my favorite episode for a few reasons.

Firstly, I love history and dream sequences. Secondly, at the end it becomes an anti-gun show. Bobby turns in his toy guns. I was hoping some of our audience would see this the way I hoped that they would when Bobby says, "All guns do is bring trouble."

The show featured Burt Mustin, an old character actor who played the grandson of Jesse James. I had always enjoyed Burt Mustin's performances and was delighted that he would be in our show.

The script described the dream sequence in which Jesse James came into a railroad car. The Brady family was all dressed in Western costumes. Jesse was brandishing a revolver. Bobby would run up to Jesse and say that the outlaw was his hero. Jesse would ignore Bobby and shoot Bobby's family, thus proving that bad guys are bad guys.

We had a big cardboard revolver made, and when Jesse would shoot the gun, he would say, "Bang, bang!" so as to make sure everyone didn't take this for real in any way. Then the Brady family would die comedic deaths.

I thought about the scene and realized that for it to work, in his head Mike Lookinland would have to see his TV family die for real. His reaction would have to be the way he was seeing it if they were really being shot, not the way they were humorously throwing themselves over each other. I asked the director, Les Martinson, if he could film this scene without rehearsal. Les knew me well enough to trust I had something unique in mind.

I told Frances Whitfield what I was doing and, though it was unorthodox, she also thought it was important enough to allow me to do what I wanted to try.

I took Mike off the set and talked to him about horrible things: about his dog being run over, about what happens to people when they really get shot. I wanted him to see the horror of violence, rather than the make-believe violence that would be going on in the scene. I didn't like what I was doing, but I didn't know any other way to achieve the effect.

The cameras rolled, and Mike came into the scene. He ran up to Jesse James as the script dictated. Then when Jesse began "shooting" the Brady family with his cartoon gun and yelling, "Bang! Bang!", Mike reacted to the horrors that I had been describing. He began yelling, "No, Jesse! Stop! That's my family!" It was chilling. When I look at the scene, I see the dichotomy of what the family is doing and what Mike is seeing, and it's truly compelling.

We filmed it in one take, and it was just what I was looking for. Following the scene, I took Mike off the set again and debriefed him, assuring him that everything was okay. Was I doing the right thing? Is it worth making a child go through a trauma for the good of a scene? I'm ambivalent. Sometimes I believe it's important enough. I know the scene and the episode say a lot and may do a small part to influence children away from violence. That much I'm proud of.

CHAPTER 42

MR. K

Every once in a while I have had to do things that were outside the norm on a set. Such was the time I got a call that we were having distinguished visitors—very distinguished visitors. One time, Nelson Rockefeller visited the set; another time, Roy Rogers. And apparently, Henry Kissinger's 10-year-old son was a big fan of *The Brady Bunch* and wanted to visit the set with his father. So one day, it became my job to show the Kissinger family around.

The first order of business was security. Even though this was the 70s and long before the super-stringent security measures of today, there still was a sweep by FBI guys to make sure the Secretary of State was safe. Then when Kissinger arrived, I showed him all around the set. The kids took his son off to show them the school room and their dressing rooms.

When Dr. Kissinger and I had some time to talk, I looked over and saw that our make-up girl was in a close conversation with one of the Secretary of State's security men. I pointed that out to Dr. Kissinger, who had a well-known reputation for being a ladies' man.

"Dr. Kissinger, it looks like one of your men is trying to pick up my make-up girl."

Kissinger looked over and commented with a laugh, "I taught him everything he knows."

Later when I was walking him back to his limo, I couldn't help but tell

Dr. Kissinger that we had another connection.

"Dr. Kissinger, when I took a poli-sci class in college, we used one of your books as a textbook."

"Oh, which one?"

I don't remember the title now, but it was written when he was professor, and it had to do with American foreign policy.

I told him, "I've got to tell you, I found it very hard reading."

Kissinger said, "One of my critics came to the same conclusion when he finished reading that book. He wrote, 'I don't know if Dr. Henry Kissinger is a good writer, but I do know that I am a good reader.'"

Kissinger laughed. I laughed too; not because I had to, but because I thought he was amusing and charming in person.

I found out by reading Jerry Stiller's autobiography, *Married to Laughter*, that Jerry's son—and now major star, Ben Stiller—came to the set when he was a child. Apparently, it was a highlight of his life when he got to meet Mike Lookinland. Ironic that many years later, he was to marry Christine Taylor who played Marcia Brady in *The Brady Bunch Movie*.

CHAPTER 43

LEAPING TO CONCLUSIONS

My poor sister, Hope, has recurring nightmares ever since she played in the memorable episode "Greg Gets Grounded," which found her at the drive-in movie with Barry Williams' Greg. You might remember the episode by its most memorable phrase—"Exact words"—which Greg used to scam his way out of being grounded.

I have always been fascinated with stunts and special effects and how they are accomplished. Just as the volcano had to explode in a previous episode, frogs had to jump onto my sister's head in this one. How would this happen?

First, we had to find the right frogs. We located huge bullfrogs that had to be removed from the set until their big scene since their loud croaking was picked up on the sensitive microphones. The same guy who brought us the frogs had brought us the tarantula that climbed on Peter during one of the Hawaii episodes. In that case, half the time it was a dead tarantula, and the other half of the time the spider wrangler placed little plastic coverings over the live tarantula's fangs. I don't know exactly what he used for the tarantula fang coverings; I can't believe there is an enormous market for those tiny implements. Anyway, this was the man you'd call when you need creepy, crawly things for movies. I wonder if this is what he always had wanted to do when he grew up.

This time he brought these enormous frogs. The plot had to deal with Greg being grounded, then being ungrounded. At the same time, Bobby had entered a frog jumping contest. Plot and subplot come together when the frogs are left in the rear seat as Greg and his date go to the drive in. My sister, Hope, has had bad luck with Greg at drive-ins before—she also played Greg's date in the episode "The Big Bet" in which Greg lost a bet to Bobby and had to cater to Bobby's every whim, which included taking his youngest brother on his date, which Bobby promptly ruined. That didn't deter lothario Greg from trying to lure her there again.

Once at the drive-in, the first camera shot was a cardboard box with the frogs in the back seat of the convertible. When Greg moves in to kiss his date, a frog is supposed to jump out of the box and land on her head.

The director, Jack Arnold, calls "Action!" The frog doesn't move. Apparently, frogs don't take direction, though they do react to a squirt gun filled with hot water. Water doesn't photograph, so when the frog was squirted, he leaped just as scripted. All we needed was the shot of the frog leaving the frame.

The next part was to see him fly out in a wider shot, then return to land on my sister's head. This was accomplished by building scaffolding over the back seat of the car. The scaffolding was T-shaped, and two special-effects men were lying on it just out of the camera shot and over my sister's head. Another unseen special-effects man lay on the floor of the back seat. He threw a frog up into the air where it was caught by one of the unseen special-effects men. The other special-effects man then dropped a different frog square onto my sister's head.

What is also unseen is the frog's release of urine into my sister's hair. Apparently frogs pee when they are traumatized. Who knew? My sister was a trooper. She endured a few takes of pissing frogs in order to complete the scene. At that point, Greg really wasn't inclined to try another move. For some reason a girl whose hair is filled with amphibian urine is a turn off.

The next part of the scene had a frog drop onto a pizza—not exactly an appetizing situation for Greg either. See what happens when a plot and subplot come together on *The Brady Bunch*?

When Hope got home that night, she shampooed her hair six times.

CHAPTER 44

A NOSE BY ANY OTHER NAME

Many people can quote Shakespeare, but more people can quote *Brady*. That's not something that is meant as self-aggrandizement, but it's just true. And among the things that people can quote is, "Oh, my nose!"

This might be the signature moment in *The Brady Bunch*. Everybody seems to know about it. I got a call from author Joe Garner who writes beautiful books on media history. He has put together titles on news events and sports events which come with CDs or DVDs. They sell very well, and he decided to write one about television called *Stay Tuned: Television's Fifty Unforgettable Moments*. He had determined that of the 50 moments, 13 were from entertainment television. The others were non-entertainment moments like the Kennedy Assassination and the Mexico Olympics, plus others from news or sports. Of the 13 entertainment moments, Marcia getting hit in the nose by the football was included.

"Oh, my nose!" ranks up there with an *I Love Lucy* moment and Sammy Davis Jr. kissing Archie Bunker in *All in the Family* and the Beatles' first American appearance on *The Ed Sullivan Show*. Amazing.

When Joe Garner called to investigate the moment and to secure the rights, he didn't know I was the one who had thrown the ball. He was elated. He wanted an interview for his book and then a DVD interview. Other people came in to see him that same day I visited his offices to do the interviews. I found myself in the company of Neil Armstrong, who had also done something rather famous.

It's funny. When you do something you consider ordinary, you don't think about it. Then, in this case, for some reason that moment has become something that people remember.

Here's what happened.

In the scene, Greg and Peter are throwing a football in the backyard. Marcia comes to the door of the family room and the ball gets away and hits her in the nose. The plot involves a hip guy who Marcia likes, quarterback Doug Simpson, who gets turned off by her swollen purple nose and breaks their date.

Earlier in the episode, Marcia had dumped the much dorkier Charley in favor of Doug, telling Charlie a little white lie to cancel the date. In fact, the line Marcia used on Charley was a line right out of my sad dating history. A few girls, not wanting to hurt my feelings, broke dates with me by using the line, "Something suddenly came up."

They always say: Write what you know. So we put "Something suddenly came up" into the script. Two times, in fact. Marcia first used it on Charley, and then, ironically, Doug used it on Marcia.

And although that line is a memorable one for Brady fans, nothing compares with "Oh, my nose!"

Anyway, when we were shooting the football scene, the ball was thrown back and forth by Peter and Greg. It was a real football. It was determined by the director, Jack Arnold, that the simplest way to get the shot of Marcia getting hit in the nose would be in a close up. A different kind of ball was substituted.

This episode was shot just before Nerf footballs were commonly used, so the "football" we used to hit her was a football-shaped piece of foam rubber that was fashioned for the occasion by the enterprising special-effects department of Paramount Studios.

After the master sequence, all that was left was the actual close-up of Marcia being hit in the nose by the football. Barry and Chris had already gone back to school, and so the job of hitting Marcia in the nose fell to our prop department. We had two older, rather non-athletic men—Irving Feinberg and Joe Kelly—who created many of the props for the series. These were not the right guys to throw the ball. We tried a couple of takes with them, but the ball didn't spiral and came nowhere close to hitting Maureen.

"Give me the ball," I said.

I had played football in pick-up games and could throw a fairly accurate pass. Jack Arnold rolled the camera, and in one take, I nailed Maureen square in the nose and landed myself in a book about the 50 greatest moments in TV history.

I've done a lot of things in my career—TV shows, theatre, movies—but I don't know if anything I will ever do will be remembered as much as that football throw. Oh, well, some people aren't remembered for anything.

CHAPTER 45

MISDIRECTED

In the second year of the show, Dad thought that Robert might soften up his antagonisms if we allowed him to direct an episode. He prepared well and did a good job directing "The Winner," an episode that featured Bobby and his desire to win a trophy.

By Season 4 Dad figured Bob deserved another shot at directing, so he was given the chance to helm "How to Succeed in Business," the episode about Peter and his ill-fated job at a bicycle store.

Maybe Robert Reed's first directing experience was beginner's luck. Maybe he just got overconfident and thought directing was so easy. Anyway, on the first day of shooting his second episode, he got into immediate trouble on a scene and started falling behind. In television the director can't fall behind. There are only so many hours in which to shoot a show, and the financial impact of not finishing is a huge black mark against any director who lets his time run out. As the day went along, Robert was losing more and more hours.

I had a conversation with Alan Rudolph, the assistant director. After his *Brady* days, Alan became a protégé of Robert Altman and has had a marvelous career as a feature film director. Alan was Oscar Rudolph's son. Oscar directed more episodes of *The Brady Bunch* than anybody else. Alan and I are contemporaries and used to get in heated philosophical discussions about the relative importance of directors and producers in television. Not surprisingly Alan believed directors more important, and I thought producers more influential.

Alan and I did share one significant similarity: Robert Reed detested both of our fathers and was vocal about it.

Both Alan's job and my job were to make sure the set ran smoothly and that we finished our work, which meant being there for the director. We were caught in an interesting situation. If we didn't help out and Robert didn't finish, he would be prevented from directing again. That was something that Alan and I would have enjoyed. On the other hand, we could do our jobs and save his skin.

We talked about it and decided to help Robert, but not until after we fantasized about how much fun it would be to just let him hang himself.

We took Robert aside. It was the first time I had seen him panicky.

"Bob, you're falling behind."

"I know."

"Why don't you just set up the shots and let us take over? You call 'Action,' but concentrate on your acting. This episode is a little too much for you right now."

He looked at us with a mixture of gratitude and wonderment. He couldn't figure out why we wanted to help him, after he had treated our fathers so badly. Trust me; we didn't want to help him. We had to do what was right for the show.

For the rest of the episode Alan and I took over and called the shots. At the end of the shoot, we had made up the lost time, and it turned out to be a good show. We were subtle enough in doing what we were doing so that no one knew what was happening.

But Robert knew. He found me after we wrapped for the day and said, "You saved my ass. I have been unkind to you, and I'm sorry about that."

I said, "Bob, you just do what you have to do."

After that, he was nice to me—for about a week.

CHAPTER 46

ONLY AS OLD AS YOU FEEL

Though we didn't do many episodes that featured the parents, we felt we owed it to Florence to give her a chance to do something unique every once in a while. That was the reason we decided to do an episode in which she and Robert played their own grandmother and grandfather, respectively.

Robert was a method actor. He dug in and created an entire background for his character and played him with a mid-European accent of some kind. I'm sure it was thoroughly accurate. He even saw to it that the character was as genetically humorless as was his grandson, Mike.

When Robert came out of make-up, he had completely transformed himself into an old man, and everyone in the crew treated him as such. They weren't instructed to do that; they just did.

When Florence came out of make-up, she was a sprightly elderly woman with a bit of a Midwest accent. Florence is from Indiana, and I think she used her background to help invent what she was doing.

In the first scene between them, Robert was filled with character. He was slow in speech and halting in his gait. I got the sense that Florence hadn't really thought through what she was going to do. By nature, Florence is a competitor, and she immediately saw Robert's attention to detail and character development as a challenge to her acting ability.

By the time the next scene took place, Florence did some homework and had really brought a whole new dimension to her character.

As the plot develops, the kids think that Grandma is just what Grandpa needs to stop his stuffy ways. It works. He is brought out of his shell.

In a lot of ways, the relationship mirrors Robert and Florence because nobody plays a stuffy, pedantic man better than Robert Reed. In real life, it didn't work. Robert never became fun loving, but as Latin-quoting stuffy grandpa, Robert Reed finally found a character who was as dry as he was. And he did a good job of acting it.

CHAPTER 47

NOT LEARNED IN FILM SCHOOL

After being an associate producer for a couple of years, once again I thought I could do more. I approached Dad before the beginning of the fourth season and told him I'd like to direct an episode. By that time, we had given several new directors their shot, including Robert Reed. I pointed out that I knew the show better than any of them, and I knew I could do a good job.

Dad agreed, and we decided that I'd direct an episode near the end of Season 4. It was the episode entitled "Room at the Top," another fan favorite in which Greg and Marcia vie for the newly created attic bedroom.

Ever financially conscious, Howard Leeds wanted me to forfeit my salary as associate producer that week. I refused. I'd be doing double duty and pointed out I'd still be doing my job unless they hired another associate producer that week. They didn't. I got both salaries. I'm not money grubbing. I just did both jobs and deserved to be paid as such.

I worked very hard preparing to direct the script. I made shot sheets and drew every angle. I'd spent over three years preparing for this opportunity. Many directors draw little sketches in their scripts alongside the scene. I took another copy of the script and made full diagrams. When Maureen approached me on the first day of filming, she saw that my script was devoid of any markings and assumed that I hadn't prepared. She spread the word among the kids who decided that they'd band together to pull me through. I heard about it and showed them my script with all the drawings, and they felt much better.

By the time I was ready to say "Action!" on my first scene, I had worked with dozens of directors. I had helped them all set their shots, worked out dolly moves and cranes shots, but I had never actually said "Action" myself. I had always wondered about how I'd say it. Some directors yell "Action!" as if they're trying to lead cheers. Some whisper "Action" to demonstrate they are quietly in command. How would I do it? I didn't know. I don't think it's anything you really prepare for. All I knew was after the camera rolled, and the sound man called, "Speed," and the actors knew their lines and were in place, it would get very quiet. And then I would say "Action" in some way that would then become my style.

The first scene I would film would be a simple one—just Barry and Maureen in the girls' bedroom. Greg would enter and find Marcia distraught. He would sit down next to her on the bed, and they would talk about the attic room into which one of them would move. We had filmed this kind of scene numerous times. Just two people in a confined set. There needn't be much camera movement. I had selected this uncomplicated scene as my first one since I was just beginning to direct.

I set the shot, rehearsed the actors, and told the assistant director to roll the camera, but he didn't. Instead, I heard a drum beat—a drum beat that was getting louder as it grew closer. Before I knew it, there was an impromptu parade in front of me. The cast had arranged the festivities to celebrate my directing debut. They had gag gifts and made sure that a good time was had by all, but I couldn't let them know that the one thing I didn't want was time taken out of my day.

I accepted each present graciously, even made some jokes about the Maalox and megaphone and jodhpurs that they gave me. Florence had a special medal made with the name of the episode and the date. It was heartfelt, appreciated and, I am sorry to say, totally unwelcome.

I went along with it. And I appreciated the sentiment deeply. Forgive me if I sound like an ingrate, but a director has to finish on time, and I started off by losing a well-intentioned hour.

Finally, they cleared the set and I got down to work. Roll camera; the sound man says "Speed;" and I say "Action." I say it quietly with a bit of upbeat energy. I guess that would be my style.

Barry enters the room, and sees Maureen on the bed. The camera pulls back and becomes a two shot. Just as rehearsed. They do all the lines right, and I say, "Cut."

When a director says "Cut!" there is a pregnant moment when the crew pauses to see if they'll do the scene again or move into close-ups or another sequence. Everyone heard the word "Cut," and surely thought that I'd move on; but I didn't. I noticed something that was added unexpectedly to the scene, and I said, "I'd like to do another one."

People were confused. It sounded all right to them. The camera work was okay. What was the problem?

The problem was that this episode was being shot at the height of the sexual tension between Barry and Maureen. When Barry sat down on the bed and started to talk to his TV sister, it became romantic, even steamy.

I couldn't print a scene in which a brother and sister were obviously hot for each other. I announced that we'd do the scene again. Nobody knew why, nor did I feel I could discuss it with anyone.

The camera moved back into place. Maureen took her place on the bed. Barry went to his place just outside the door. The camera rolled. The sound man called, "Speed." I said, "Action." Barry entered and sat on the bed next to Maureen. Once again, the lines were right. And once again, steam from the two of them.

This definitely was not anything I learned to deal with in my production classes at UCLA. The question "What do you do when your teenage stars who are playing brother and sister are horny for each other?" just never came up on a test.

Maybe no one else on the crew was paying attention, since the words sounded right and there were no glaring errors or anything worthy of an outtake reel, but I couldn't let it go like that. Everyone looked at me, and I said, "We're going to do it again."

Normally on a filmed TV series, a scene will be finished in three or four takes. Sometimes even one or two. In a particularly involved scene, it can go five or six. Economics dictate that any more than that, and you're in difficulty of not finishing the show on time.

We went three, four, five, six, seven, eight, nine, ten, eleven, and then twelve takes. Once or twice a line was flubbed, and sometimes a camera move wasn't quite smooth, but most of them looked and sounded fine—to everybody else. What was I going to do? These two teenagers were lusting for each other, and I was getting it on film.

I couldn't say anything to Barry or Maureen. That would have been far too humiliating. I wracked my brain, and suddenly remembered a psychology class I had taken in college. The teacher had discussed psychic distance. Psychic distance meant a physical barrier between two people which creates distance emotionally as well. That was it.

I went to Barry and asked him to change the blocking. I told him that it would be better for the camera if he placed his arm straight down between Maureen and himself. He agreed. We shot the scene. Psychic distance worked. Barry and Maureen cooled down just enough, and Greg and Marcia's relationship was entirely appropriate once again.

Luckily, every other sequence went much more easily. I finished on time, and had a ball. The network reported that they liked it so much that they wanted me to do more episodes, but I wanted to focus my energies on becoming a producer, which happened the next season.

In my role as associate producer, it was my post-production job to work with the editors and dub the film. Dubbing is where the dialogue track and sound-effects track and music tracks are mixed together. It is also where the laugh track is added. It's a very coordinated creative effort to get the sound just right.

I confess that the laugh track on the Brady episode I directed is significantly louder than any of the other episodes. I'm a little embarrassed about it now, but I wanted to make sure that the manufactured audience got all the jokes I directed. By the way, the scene between Barry and Maureen had very few laughs.

CHAPTER 48

A DAY IN THE LIFE OF *THE BRADY BUNCH*

Many people ask what a day is like on a TV show. For me, I had just come out of college, so Paramount was like another campus. It was like going to school early. And since most of every day was spent inside Stage Five, I rarely saw the sun. I would always get to work around 6:15 a.m., before any of the actors. And then I would always be the last person to leave the show at the end of the day, when the sun was down again.

Many producers and associate producers arrive after the actors get through putting on their make-up, but I always wanted to beat the cast to the studio. It's a habit I have maintained since I was a dialogue coach on *The Brady Bunch*. I have always felt that since the performers are called that early, someone from the producers' office should be there to let the actors know that someone is there who is on their side.

Of course, I wasn't being completely magnanimous. I had an alternative reason. My social life was almost nonexistent since I was locked away from dating possibilities most of every day. While the kids' make-up was done on the stage, Florence had her make-up done in the make-up department where the other shows' stars were also being made up. I made a habit of casually dropping by to "check on" Florence. One of the shows at Paramount at that time was

Love: American Style, and each week there were new attractive women who I could accidentally bump into. My plan actually worked a couple of times.

Anyway, the set started to come to life around 6:30 a.m. The call sheets were handed out, which had the day's work listed. A normal episode would have a 35-page script. Each scene was divided into eighths. For example, the call sheet would list who was in the scene and then say that a scene was being played in the living room and was 3 3/8 pages. At the beginning of the series, a show would take four days to film. Therefore there would be approximately 8 1/2 pages a day.

A few years into the show the studio, to save money, tightened the schedule. For a period of six episodes, we did them in 2 1/2 days—or two episodes per week. It proved to be very grinding, and so we went back to our usual schedule.

Later, also for a few episodes, the studio—again to save money—arbitrarily asked us to eliminate one of the six kids from each episode on a rotating basis. We did it for a short while, but Dad talked the studio out of this since he knew the audience had their favorites and would miss the missing Brady kid.

Because of the six kids, the schedule had to revolve around the hours they were allowed to work. The state of California is strict. Not only can children only work 10 hours a day, their work could not be done after 6:30 p.m. Our schedule staggered the kids' camera time so they could get in their required three hours of school. It also meant that adult scenes would be shot at the end of the day after the kids had left.

Every morning when the cast would arrive, and after donuts and coffee at craft service, they would confirm with me what the day's work would be. If an actor wasn't in any of the scenes that day, they would be "on hold," and not come in at all unless the schedule changed. If an actor were in a scene later in the day, he or she would get a later call. The previous night, the second assistant director would make sure they all had call sheets and knew what scenes to study.

After going over the scenes with the director and camera man, I would then check with Frances Whitfield to let her know if there was anything unusual regarding the kids that might call for her to bank school hours. When all were gathered before shooting it was a time for socializing, but more importantly, I would make sure that each of them was ready for the day's filming. That meant ensuring that they knew their lines and answering any questions they might have. It might also mean on-set rewriting in case there was difficulty with their lines.

The parents, usually the mothers, were close by, and I was always available to them if there were any special requests. It was almost a club for them, and they grew very close. Florence and Ann would rarely leave the set, though they both had dressing rooms on the stage in the back. Both of the women took up needlepointing, and they always could be found close by if they were in the scene. Robert would only come out when called from his dressing room. It was long before cellular phones, so that was never a distraction.

The alleyway just off the set was where Paramount had built the school room. As some of the kids got older, a new teacher, Beth Clopton, was added for secondary schools, and another school room was created. The kids' dressing rooms also lined the alley. When Barry reached 18, he was accorded some additional privileges, like an inside dressing room and the right to call the directors by their first names.

My on-set work then turned to working with the director. Since we used rotating directors, they were often new to the series, and I would fill them in on how we usually would shoot the set—the particular angles and lighting problems. Also, I would let them know what they could expect from each of the actors, and especially how to talk to Robert Reed.

By lunch, I could tell how the day was going, and whether the director was ahead or behind. That would mean decisions had to be made about the rest of the schedule. We could add a scene if ahead, and the actors and crew would have to be told to be ready for it. If we were behind, I would call the office and let Sherwood know in case something could be cut or shortened or moved to another set so it wouldn't take as long.

On the set I never called Dad "Dad." I always referred to him or addressed him as "Sherwood." It's not that everyone didn't know he was my father. I never tried to keep that a secret, as if I could. It's just that I felt it was bad form to be saying or calling out "Dad," in a professional situation.

By the end of the day, we would finish the work. In all five years of *The Brady Bunch*, we only went over schedule half of one day. Being in production, I am extremely proud of that.

While all this is happening on the set for a given episode, other things are going on relating to other episodes. In the office, Dad, Howard, and a story editor would be breaking new stories or rewriting scripts. Editors were working on previous episodes. It would normally take nine weeks from production to go through post-production, which included editing, dubbing, and prints.

Today most TV shows are edited on video, so the process is more streamlined.

Filming is exhausting, and I rarely sat down. One of our cinematographers, Les Schorr, even had special shoes molded so he could cope with the standing easier.

Set time is the most expensive cost of a set. Everything had to be ready so when the director calls "Action!" it is a smooth operation. If someone isn't there, or a special effect or a prop isn't ready, or an actor isn't prepared, the clock ticks loudly and expensively.

And no one wants to be blamed if we go over. That time demand has led to "set talk"—or in other words, a way for people to cover their asses. For example, if someone asks somebody on the set, "What time is it?" The answer is never "Two-thirty." It's "According to my watch, it's two-thirty." That way you can blame your watch if you get the time wrong. Or, "Did you see Chris?" The answer isn't "He's by craft service." It's "The last time I saw him, he was at craft service." That way, if he moved, you can't be held responsible. It's a phenomenon, and people just fall into it.

And using "set talk," *according to my computer*, this chapter is over.

CHAPTER 49

GRIMM STORY

We always tried to kick off the season with something out of the ordinary. That's the reason the series had three-parters in the Grand Canyon (Season 3) and Hawaii (Season 4). For the start of Season 5, we didn't have a trip planned. Instead, we thought we'd pay homage to the classic fairy tale, *Snow White and the Seven Dwarfs*.

A script was written, and we went to work on deciding which kid would be which dwarf. All we knew for sure was that Jan should be Grumpy. While this was going on, we heard the first rumblings about Disney's territorial ownership of the fairy tale. Though *Snow White* was written by the Brothers Grimm over a hundred years ago, in the Disney animated version Walt had made some classic changes. Most significant was to give the seven dwarfs names. Sleepy, Dopey, Doc, Bashful, Happy, Grumpy, and Sneezy were created by the Disney Company and were trademarked. *Snow White* was public domain, but Disney owns the names of the Dwarfs.

We contacted the Disney Company and asked if we could use the names. We didn't hear anything, and we started getting closer to our shooting date. These kinds of issues historically take a long time as lawyers get into it.

Dad didn't know what to do. And I felt badly. The idea of doing the show was mine, and now I was feeling that I had saddled us with a problem we couldn't solve since we weren't hearing from the Disney Company.

I really liked the colorful nature of the episode, with each of the kids as a dwarf and adding Sam to give us seven, and with Carol as Snow White, Mike as the Handsome Prince, and Alice as the wicked queen. We were giving ourselves a chance to have a lot of fun, if Disney would just let us. Corporations don't care if we have fun or not. They are always watching out for their bottom line, and it didn't do them any good for us to co-opt their character names for our show. But why didn't they just tell us that, so we could move on?

My argument was that we were honoring their show by poking fun at the movie, but apparently they weren't seeing it that way. In fact, they didn't see it *any* way since we didn't hear anything from the Mickey Mouse company, and we were getting ever closer to filming something that we weren't technically being allowed to film.

If we filmed without their okay, they could sue us, and Paramount doesn't take kindly to lawsuits. We were in a quandary.

At the same time, one added bit of fun that we might be forced to give up was our use of Frances Whitfield, playing herself, in the episode. Our beloved school teacher was as much a part of the Brady family as any of the parents of the kids. The story of "Snow White and the Seven Bradys" involved the Brady family putting on the play to raise money to buy a retirement gift for their favorite teacher. Frances was thrilled to dust off her Screen Actors Guild card to play the part of the teacher herself—that is, if Disney would let us do it at all.

We went blithely ahead, always believing that Disney would grant permission. After all, in fairy tales things have to turn out happily ever after.

But it wasn't until two days before filming that we received the word that we could do it! It was reported to us that there was a large corporate committee meeting about it in New York. Arguments were made for and against allowing *The Brady Bunch* to use the names of the dwarfs. Finally, the head attorney looked at everyone and gave his most sage opinion: "You know something? I don't give a shit about this."

We took that as an okay and did the show.

CHAPTER 50

DUTCH TREAT

In the fourth season, the Brady kids recorded a Christmas album and were invited onto *The Merv Griffin Show* to sing a carol. This talk show was a short-lived nighttime version of Merv's long-running daytime show which CBS scheduled to challenge *The Tonight Show Starring Johnny Carson*. I was asked to accompany the Brady kids unofficially. From time to time, like my experiences with Barry, I served as guardian for their activities off the set.

We were all waiting in a green room at CBS Television City when I asked one of the show staff who the other guests were. I was told: Jose Feliciano and Ronald Reagan. At that time, Reagan was no longer Governor of California, but he continued to be an important national figure. There was even talk of his running for President. The kids and their parents were excited that they could possibly meet Reagan. Most of the Brady kids and their families were politically conservative, and he was their hero.

Ronald Reagan wasn't mine. Besides leaning left while I was at UCLA, I had mourned when Reagan had cut many of the programs at the university, and he was not the darling of most of the students.

Susan's Olsen's mother asked me, "Do you think you could introduce us to the Governor?"

I answered quickly, "No. This isn't my show," thereby getting me out of any responsibility to have to be around such a meeting.

I felt fine with my position until Eve Plumb, knowing my political persuasion, said, "If he was a Democrat, you'd find a way."

"That's probably right."

I was okay with my answer—for awhile. Then I began to regret bringing my own politics into the mix. I slipped out of the room and went down a small hallway toward another green room.

I opened the door and went inside. Ronald Reagan was completely alone. When you are not in political office, you aren't assigned bodyguards. He looked up and saw me. I got right to the point.

"Mr. Reagan, would you come with me please?"

Not seeming to be inquisitive as to who I was, he said, "Sure."

He probably thought I was an assistant on *The Merv Griffin Show* as we walked down the hallway. I looked over at him and thought to myself, "If I were another kind of person. . . ."

I quickly got any of those kinds of thoughts out of my head, and instead I realized how fragile our system is and how difficult it is to protect our leaders, and how we have to value the people who take on the responsibility of being our statesmen, especially if we don't agree with them.

My musings were interrupted when Reagan asked, "Where are we going?"

"The *Brady Bunch* kids wanted to meet you."

He answered, "Good. I watch that show all the time."

I guess our series was reaching all kinds of audiences. I started to think about him at his home, hearing the theme song and calling into the kitchen, "Nancy, come quick! *The Brady Bunch* is on."

And Nancy would grab a bowl of popcorn, and they'd snuggle on the couch and watch Mike and Carol solve a simple problem—a problem which he'd remember later and would use to solve a world crisis in a simple way. We did an episode where Peter and Greg divided their room with a line of masking tape during a fight. Do you think Reagan remembered that Brady incident when he said, "Mr. Gorbachev, tear down this wall?"

Anyway, I brought Ronald Reagan into the room and said simply, "Kids, this is Governor Reagan."

He chatted with them a while. I knew I had done the right thing, and as far as I was concerned: The far-right thing.

CHAPTER 51

JOE WILLIE

I don't get nervous talking to movie stars or politicos. But sports stars? I get a little tongue-tied. When we did an episode about a football star, we were able to cast Joe Namath. It was just a couple of years after his incredible upset victory with the Jets over the Colts in the Super Bowl, and he was still everyone's football hero.

The episode "Mail Order Hero" featured Bobby's tall tale about having a serious illness, which he and Cindy hoped would compel the football star to visit him. The story was a completely original idea. Nowadays, writing staffs develop stories for shows by finding ways to twist episodes that they've seen before. Maybe that's a product of television being over 50 years old, but I think it shows a serious lack of creativity and a lack of respect for the creative process to settle for something that's already been done.

On the contrary, when Dad, Howard, the story editor, and I would get together to discuss a story idea, we would reject it if we'd seen a show like it. That is not to say that all of our episodes were ablaze with creativity, but we never deliberately copied anything.

One of the most original shows was our episode with Joe Namath. We were sitting in the office trying to figure out a way to get a celebrity into an episode in a unique (but logical) manner. That was our task, and we put that question to ourselves. How would we, ourselves, be able to accomplish it? Better yet, how would a kid manage to get a star to come to his house? It came to us just like it came to Bobby and Cindy in the episode. I had seen in the news that actor Mike Connors (*Mannix*) did a bit of charity visiting a children's hospital and was happy to be there for the kids. What if Bobby pretended he was dying? Would that work? Would that lure a good-hearted star? Of course it would. Since we didn't want to be too morbid, we decided that Bobby wouldn't pretend to be dying; he'd just pretend to be very sick.

It also enabled us to have great fun at the end of the episode when Mike, not aware of his children's scheme, arrives home to find Joe Namath in his living room. Namath is very concerned about Bobby whereas Mike Brady, thinking Bobby merely has a cold, says "Hey, things like this happen" with a smile.

Of course, the Brady kids learn a valuable lesson about lying and what happens. But I also learned something—that trying to come up with an episode is easier if you merely ask yourself, "What would I do?"

Having Namath on the set was great fun. Florence, being Florence, even threw herself into his arms. Everybody went up to talk football, just like we all had talked baseball with Don Drysdale in a previous episode. I even got a great picture of me showing Joe Namath how to throw a pass.

I also had the chance to take him aside and ask him the all-important question: "How are the Jets going to do this year?"

Joe smiled and said, "We're going to win it all again."

I went home after filming and found a bookie and put money on the Jets because I had inside info from Joe Namath.

The Jets went four and ten.

CHAPTER 52

YOU FIT THE SUIT

Though "Oh, my nose!" and "Marcia, Marcia, Marcia!" and "Pork chops and applesauce" and "Mom always said: 'Don't play ball in the house'" are all readily identifiable to most fans as being from *The Brady Bunch*, the Brady phrase that Dad and I like best is, "You fit the suit."

Can you remember what episode that's from? Many people can't. It's from "Adios Johnny Bravo." The Season 5 episode even spawned a cartoon series. But we always have most appreciated the episode for its key line—"You fit the suit"—and the philosophical implications the line offers.

Briefly: Greg is lured into the Bradyized version of heavy rock and roll. He had been performing with his brothers and sisters, but a record producer spotted Greg and says he can make Greg a big star if he would abandon his siblings and go solo. The record company gives a big push to get him on their label. They want to change his image, have him wear a fancy bullfighter-type suit (which actually was a bullfighter suit we found in the Paramount wardrobe department), and rename Greg Brady, "Johnny Bravo." Quite a dilemma for loyal Greg: Be true to his siblings or become a big rock star. Finally, the other kids decide that they don't want to stand in Greg's way for fame and fortune and tell him that he should go for it.

Greg records a demo, and when the hot A&R woman (former Playmate of the Year Claudia Jennings) plays it back for him, his voice is barely audible through all the overdubs and echoes and background vocals. Greg is confused. Why did they love him so much if his voice can't even be heard?

The promoter says, "That's easy, man: You fit the suit."

Of course, what the promoter meant was that the record company had come up with this persona—Johnny Bravo—that was the name and suit. They just needed to find some random, decent-looking "Johnny Doe" who fit into it, and Greg fit the bill.

Though we are proudest of the moral of the episode, the decision to do the show was not based on any lesson to be learned . . . but on the fact that we wanted to do another episode where the kids sang. The audience really responded to those. At that time, Barry was really getting into music, and it was a way to feature him, too. It accomplished many things. I guess it fit our suit.

Since that episode, whenever Dad and I come up against something where things are decided for a capricious reason, we look at each other and say, "You fit the suit."

In the episode, upon hearing this, Greg physically tears up his contract. Too bad that can't be done quite so simply in real life. Anyone who tries ends up with a different kind of suit—a lawsuit.

CHAPTER 53

GOATS AND BEARS

Write what you know. Produce what you know. Dad brought family into what he knew, but when I worked on *The Brady Bunch*, I had yet to have a family. I represented the kids' point of view. He represented the parents' point of view, and it mixed well. Since that time, I have had a family of my own, and my style of parenting isn't the same as his but, all in all, I think that parenting a la Mike and Carol Brady offers a pretty good pair of role models.

From my own experience I injected some things that might not have been there if I weren't there. For one: school extracurricular activities. I had always been pretty active at school. I had run for office, like Greg and Marcia did—against each other!—in the episode "Vote for Brady." I had been a school safety officer, so Bobby got the job in the classic episode, "Law and Disorder." I had been a yell leader at UCLA, so school cheers and pompon girls would pop up in various episodes, and it was up to me to come up with routines and yells, like the rather simple cheer I invented:

"One, two, tell me who are you . . . The Bears!

"Three four, tell me who's gonna score . . . The Bears!"

Okay, I admit that it isn't a brilliant cheer, but it did seem appropriate. Another one I borrowed from UCLA was Bobby's cheer that starts, "Give me a B."

And his family says, "B!"

Then Bobby says, "Give me another B."

Again they say "B!"

Bobby says again, "Give me another B."

And they say, "B!"

Then Bobby says, "What does that spell?"

They don't know, so he puts his fingers to his lips and says, "Bubabubabub."

I hope Dad didn't think my college tuition went to waste.

I also had been a bit incorrigible. During my senior year at UCLA, I had managed to disrupt the big UCLA/USC football game by sneaking into the USC marching band and ruining the halftime show, so school pranks were not outside my area of expertise. The plot in the episode "Getting Greg's Goat"—when Greg pilfered the rival school's mascot, Raquel the goat, and hid her in his room—was exactly my kind of thing. The episode was also significant because it garnered *The Brady Bunch* its only award while it was on the air. Though we had never won an Emmy in any category, or a People's Choice Award, we triumphed at the Patsy Awards (the American Humane Association awards for animal actors) when Raquel took home the gold for best performance by a goat.

We had been to the Grand Canyon; we had been to Hawaii. In the fifth season, what could we ever do to top those scenic places? Of course: Cincinnati. I admit—with all due respect to Cincinnati—it seemed like a bit of a comedown, but the cast and crew had a good time.

We were contacted by the amusement park, King's Island, which presented us with the following deal: If we filmed an episode there, they would cover any overages beyond what a regular episode might cost.

Why not?

For the episode, "Cincinnati Kids," we concocted a storyline in which Mike was hired to design a building or something for the park, and the family would tour the park while he was safely out of the fun at a meeting. Mike's plans—secured in a poster tube—got mixed-up with Jan's poster of Yogi Bear, and there was a big sequence in which the whole family scoured the park to find the missing plans.

King's Island placed *The Brady Bunch* squarely in the heart of Brady-audience territory, and the cast had to be protected from its legion of fans while we were filming on location. It was pretty intense. Also intense was the large roller coaster. We were told that it was so scary that Neil Armstrong refused to ride it. Bob Reed wouldn't either.

In order to shoot people on a roller coaster, the camera man would have to be in the car in front and ride backwards while maneuvering a heavy camera. I had ridden the roller coaster to see what it would be like for the cast. At least that was my acknowledged excuse, since in truth I just love roller coasters.

On my test ride, I saw a sign that indicated that standing up is dangerous. I knew that the camera mount was about as tall as a standing person, so I suggested a trial run to see how dangerous it might be.

They tied off the camera and sent it through. The camera never came back, and the camera operator thanked me for saving his life. After getting the spare camera and rigging it lower and safer, the Brady family, sans Mr. Brady, rode the coaster without further incident.

For the episode, we needed to cast a few roles, but casting a union actor would mean we would then have to pay for room and travel. Luckily, our new dialogue coach, Bobby Hoffman, was also an actor and could cover a role. Another part could be played by Les Martinson, our director, who had been an actor. We would bring one actress, Hillary Thompson, to play Greg's love interest for that episode. All we were lacking was the role of a park mascot—a large, friendly cartoonish bear—to be played by a twenty-something guy.

I went through the crew list to see if there was anybody who could do it, and could find only one person of that age and type: Me.

I had taken an acting class and had been working with actors. I had been a stand-up comedian briefly. How tough could it be to do one scene?

We had done most of the filming, and the time came for my scene. I had done some research and interviewed an actual park mascot to see if there was anything I should be aware of to help my character. The only thing he advised was to wear an athletic cup since kids loved to punch or kick him in that area. Fortunately, I didn't have to worry since I wouldn't be out in the public.

The scene involved Greg Brady approaching a park mascot as he was looking for Marge, his King's Island girlfriend. He would talk to me, the mascot. I would answer. I would take off my bear head, and then we would finish the conversation before he ran off.

I did the scene exactly as written. No mistakes. It was printed in one take with no close-ups. We left King's Island after we all had a great time—even Robert Reed, presumably, because he didn't have to ride the roller coaster.

When we returned to the studio and edited the film, I watched my scene critically. Indeed, I did everything right. I watched a guy walk up to another actor. In the bear suit, he talked; he listened. He took off the head. He talked; he listened. Cut.

But I learned a lot. There's more to acting than doing it all right. I forgot the whole thing. I was doing it by the numbers, and that is what I saw. Nobody else seemed to notice my less-than-stellar performance, but I did. And I concluded that acting is best left to actors. However, I sincerely advise anyone who writes, produces, or directs, to act at least once. You'll gain a whole new respect for what actors have to do.

CHAPTER 54

UNRAVELING

Just as the Brady kids began their singing careers without our knowledge (or consent), they began to explore a change in their management and/or agents. Over the summer of 1973, just before we began filming Season 5, they all decided that a guy named Harvey Shotz should represent them. Neither Dad nor I had ever heard of Harvey Shotz. He had never been involved in the show in any way, but somehow he was able to get all the kids and their parents to go with him for representation.

Certainly, performers have the right to sign with anyone as their representatives, but it was a big surprise when Dad got a call from this Harvey Shotz who said he now represented all the kids and asked for a meeting.

I wasn't present at the initial lunch when Harvey told Dad that the kids wanted a lot more money, approval of storylines, and much more.

"After all, they are the real stars of a hit TV show, and they deserve salaries that represent just how huge they are," Shotz said.

Dad asked Harvey if he knew the Neilsen ratings. Harvey didn't. Of course, Dad was aware that the show was only a marginal hit in prime time, and any salary demands might get us cancelled. Harvey didn't know that. It became apparent to Dad that Harvey believed all the nonsense that he was selling the kids.

Harvey Shotz requested a face-to-face meeting with us, the kids, their parents, and himself. I was invited into a meeting with a lot of people with whom I had grown extremely close and this man whom I had never met.

Suddenly, Harvey Shotz got up and started making demands—the same kind of demands that he had made to Dad earlier. He was saying things that I knew were untrue. He said that I never took into account what the kids wanted. But I always had; I had always been there for them in every way. In disbelief, I looked at the kids who averted my eyes. I couldn't believe what I was hearing.

He capped it with: "From now on, anything you say to the kids, you'll say through me."

What? Who was this guy? I had never seen him before, and he was advocating changing how we have been doing the show.

I am not shy, not when I think I am unjustly accused.

"Why?" I asked.

He said, "Why what?"

"Why do I have to go through you to talk to the kids? I never have before, and everybody has gotten along well."

I turned to the kids. "Haven't we?"

They looked away. They were clearly becoming uncomfortable with being placed in the middle.

Harvey said, "But you don't listen to them."

This was too much. He had obviously sold them a bill of goods, and he was now using them to implement his ambitions.

I looked at the kids and said, "I'd like one example when I didn't listen to any of you."

Not one of them said anything as they looked back at our years together to try to remember any example.

Finally Harvey prodded Chris who, rather reluctantly, said, "There was this time when I wanted to say something one way and Lloyd thought I should say it the way it was in the script."

I said to Chris, "Did I listen?"

"Yes."

"That's my job. I have to decide if something is right or wrong. Most of the time, I try to incorporate what you all want. I even ask for it; don't I?"

All of them said, "Yes."

The meeting disintegrated immediately. Before they even left the building, three of them fired Harvey Shotz. However, dissension had entered the show, and much of the entire fifth and final year of the show was filmed with an us-against-them mentality. I can't even remember who stayed with Harvey Shotz and who left, but it was unpleasant for all concerned.

None of Harvey Shotz's "demands" were ever addressed. You know the expression: "If it's not broke, don't fix it." And it wasn't broken until he came along.

For the last year of the show, I was now in a Cold War relationship with these kids who had become such an integral part of my life. It shows what can happen when dreams of money fill people's heads. As far as Chris Knight was concerned, not only did it change the nature of his relationship with me, but it changed his relationship with his own mother who was one of the leaders of the pro-Harvey Shotz faction. He later told me that he felt manipulated, and his relationship with his mother was made more difficult for him.

Though they were all under contract and did the work, the good feeling of the previous four years was changed unalterably.

CHAPTER 55

BEGINNING OF THE END/ END OF THE BEGINNING

Besides the rift that was developing, the kids were getting older. The series was beginning to show its age. It was the middle of Season 5 and the network wanted to freshen up the show by adding a character.

The expression "Jump the shark" was originated when the popular TV series *Happy Days* dried up creatively. It specifically refers to an episode in which Fonzie had to jump over a shark tank on a motorcycle. By all accounts, the scene was completely unbelievable and it compromised the Fonzie character and the show's integrity so badly that it became obvious the end was near. Therefore, "Jump the shark" is now a euphemism for the last gasp of a dying series. For *The Brady Bunch*, many people think it was the arrival of Cousin Oliver that caused our show to "Jump the shark."

Though Robbie Rist was (and is) a good actor and played the character Oliver just the way we wanted him to, he threw off the balance of the show and was perceived by the audience as an interloper in the family they knew so well. The last six episodes of the series were spent integrating him into the family and setting up the changes that would have to be made in the next year with Greg going to college and Cousin Oliver supposedly giving us younger stories once again. It didn't really work all that well.

The last episode of the original series was particularly contentious because of Robert Reed. He was at his worst. The story had to do with Bobby selling hair tonic to make money. When applied, some of the users' hair turned green. Bob objected, even though Dad had researched similar cases and was told that this was possible. Dad changed the script so that some users' hair turned orange to make it more palatable to our resident skeptic and factophile Robert. He didn't respond to the changes in the script.

A side note: Dad likes to think that Forrest Gump's box-of-chocolates philosophy applies to TV filming: "Shooting a TV show is like a box of chocolates. On any shooting day, you never know what you're going to get."

So instead of Robert showing up to film at 7:30 in the morning, Dad was just out of the shower at home when he received a call from Merritt Blake, Robert's agent. Merritt informed Dad that Robert had decided not to do the episode. He had written another one of his familiar diatribes to the studio which ended with his firm declaration: "And that is why I cannot do the episode."

Robert's big complaint this time was that hair tonic can't do that to hair. Dad, knowing Robert's fact-checking obsession, had checked with Clairol's legal department who reluctantly reported that indeed sometimes that can happen with some small cheap company—not theirs, of course. Dad was scientifically and comedically correct, but not to Robert Reed's satisfaction.

Indeed I was given a copy of Robert's telegram on the set with his chemical analysis of hair tonic. We were about to film but there was no Mike Brady. I called Dad, who by that time was already coming up with a solution.

"If he can't be in it, he won't be in it."

Dad had already checked with Hank Coleman at Paramount who agreed to eliminate Robert from the episode. By the end of the fifth season, Paramount was just as sick of Robert's complaining as we were. When Dad told me all this, I could hear him smile over the phone. He told me to move to a scene that Mike Brady was not in.

I checked in with the director, Jack Arnold, to let him know what was up.

I talked to Florence and Ann B. who agreed to step in and assume all of Robert's lines. Dad was more honest with them later, telling them that Bob was completely unreasonable, even intentionally waiting until the morning of filming to draw a line in the hair tonic.

Florence and Ann B., total pros that they are, quickly learned their new lines and were ready to shoot.

We started with a scene with just the kids, and by the time Dad reached the studio he had finished the rewrite.

Where was Robert Reed during all this? He was in his trailer waiting for us to go to him with new scenes which would fundamentally change the script.

We didn't.

For the next day or two, he would come out of his trailer and walk to the set where he would stand in the eye line of the actors while they did work that he had refused to do.

Dad approached him and asked why he was on the set when he wasn't in the episode.

Bob said, "*The Brady Bunch* is my show, and I'm interested in what goes on in my show."

Dad said, "Thanks for your interest. But it's going to be distracting to the actors while we're shooting. You're standing right next to the camera and they can't help but see you."

Bob said, "I'm not saying anything," and refused to move.

The word got back to the head of the studio who, knowing about what was happening on the set, asked Dad if he wanted security to come to have Bob removed forcibly.

Dad told Hank, "You'll have to shoot me before I'll allow that. What are the kids supposed to think? Their dad, Mr. Brady, is being carried away from the set by security guards? What did he do? Is he being arrested? I don't like this man, but I like the kids, and I don't want them to see this happening right in front of them."

Fortunately and eventually, Robert realized his cause was lost, gave up his vigil, and left.

We didn't know it at the time, but this would be the last episode that *The Brady Bunch* ever filmed, and Mike Brady wasn't in it. Not only was his heart not in it, he wasn't either. People have spoken to me about the episode, and no one has ever mentioned that they didn't realize Robert Reed wasn't in it.

Meanwhile, Barry Diller had become head of ABC, and we knew he wasn't disposed to family shows. Even so, our ratings were holding up, and there was a good chance of the series going into a sixth season. That meant contracts with all the actors would have to be negotiated. And that meant we were looking at an extension for Robert Reed. Meetings were held, and it was decided if the show came back, Robert Reed wouldn't. He would be replaced as the father.

I confess: It would have been a pleasure to go to the studio and not see him. One time, Robert had been asked what he would do when *The Brady Bunch* went off the air. He replied, "Penance."

I was at my parents' home when Dad made a call to Robert's agent, Merritt Blake. Dad thinks it is unfair to blindside people.

"Merritt, this is Sherwood."

"Hey, I wondered when you'd be calling. It looks like *The Brady Bunch* may get picked up."

"That's right, but I wanted you to be the first to know: If we get picked up, Robert won't be coming back."

Merritt was stunned. As an agent, he gets a percentage of his client's salary, and if Robert is out, that's good-bye to a large amount of money.

"What do you mean: Not coming back? He's Mr. Brady. How can you do the show without Mr. Brady?"

"I didn't say Mr. Brady wouldn't be coming back. I just said Robert wouldn't. Robert has made it plain that he has been unhappy with the limitations of the role. We just felt we should relieve him of his unhappiness and allow him to explore all the other roles that he wants to. He did a great five years, and he's fulfilled his contract."

Merritt Blake didn't know what to say.

Finally, he said, "This is it? This is a final decision."

"Yes."

After a second or two to think about his client list, Merritt said, "How about John McMartin?"

So much for an agent's loyalty.

It wasn't going to be John McMartin. It wasn't going to be anybody.

Barry Diller cancelled the show. We found out about it at a luncheon that Dad and I were attending. Also at the luncheon was Bruce Lansbury, the new Vice President of Programming for Paramount TV. We knew they were in the middle of negotiating for the sixth season, so when Bruce came over to us we thought he might have some news.

He did. He said, "We fought the good fight."

That was it. Five years of the series, and it was over and done in five words.

At least we had an answer. Usually people find out about cancellation by reading about it in *Variety* or *The Hollywood Reporter*. I went back to my office and cleaned out all the things I had accumulated and put everything into boxes. I hugged my secretary, Mary Anna, good-bye and put my key on the desk.

As I walked out of the studio, I thought about how formative my five years had been. I had gone from dialogue coach to producer and director. I had gone from single and dating to being engaged to Barbara.

For all intents and purposes, I assumed *The Brady Bunch* was over.

I should have realized that *The Brady Bunch* is a lot of things, but *over* isn't one of them.

PART 3

The Brady Legacy

INTRODUCTION

By all TV standards, a five-year run of a series is a big success. At the outset of any TV project, if a producer was magically given the choice to see his or her show stay on the air for five years—no more and no less—likely 99 out of 100 would take that deal.

And when the original run of *The Brady Bunch* ended, we were gratified with the success we'd achieved, and we were pleased with our work as we started looking for the next idea to be a series.

Little did we know that there was a whole other life awaiting the Brady phenomenon—a life that would take it directions that we never imagined.

CHAPTER 56

DANCING AS FAST AS THEY COULD

If you ever run into me and ask me about *The Brady Bunch Variety Hour*, I won't know much about it. And there's a good reason: Neither my father nor I had anything to do with it. We didn't even know it was going to be on.

One day I was looking through *TV Guide* and saw that *The Brady Bunch* kids were going to be guest stars on *The Donny and Marie Show*. This was a couple of years after our series went off, and I didn't know that they could even do this legally. I called Dad and asked if he knew anything about it. He didn't either. Did they actually have the right to go on another show and call themselves *The Brady Bunch*? No. Dad owned the characters.

We watched the show and, to tell the truth, they performed okay. And okay enough to garner high ratings and an order for a *Brady Bunch Variety Hour*.

This, too, was a surprise when we read about it. Being guest stars on somebody else's show was one thing, but an entire series without contacting Sherwood Schwartz who created and produced the series?! Surely, they wouldn't have the nerve.

They would and did. Dad's attorney got involved and found out that Paramount and ABC had made a deal for the series, and Sid and Marty Kroft agreed to be the producers—on the condition that the Kroft Brothers were completely in charge—and we (in the words of Samuel Goldwyn) were "included out."

Dad was given some money to let this happen. Why didn't he fight it? He didn't need the money, but keeping the Brady franchise alive was important; it would help the syndicated run; and most importantly the actors could make significant money, and he didn't want to stop them.

I was more upset than he was. How could all these people we knew be that conspiratorial? None of us had heard a word about this from any of our actors.

I remembered once again what Oscar Rudolph had said: "Never trust an actor."

I considered it a double cross. To specifically exclude the people who were responsible for *The Brady Bunch* and who had created and produced the series and, keep it a secret while they were doing it, was high treason.

They went ahead and did the first episode. When I tried to watch the premiere, I was suddenly happy no one ever talked to us about doing the show.

I wanted to watch the hour as a viewer might. I did my best to be objective. I saw people doing a bad impression of a variety show. They weren't professional singers and dancers, and they tried their best to do production numbers that they were simply ill-equipped to do. They were doing sketch comedy, but they lacked that special kind of comic skill. Then there were other dancers and a swimming pool, and I didn't know why. I couldn't make sense of the whole show, and I found it unfunny and not entertaining in the slightest.

Was I bitter that they did the show without us? Sure. But, in spite of how it all came about and the basic duplicity, I still can distinguish between a good show and the disaster I was witnessing.

I was able to watch half of one episode before I turned off the TV. I left the room and was happy and proud that I had nothing to do with it. I never watched it again, and it was cancelled after six episodes.

But even that catastrophe couldn't bury the *Bunch*.

CHAPTER 57

RETURN OF THE BUNCH

For me, a lot went on between the end of the original series in 1974 and 1981. After *The Brady Bunch* went off the air, I raised the money and made a movie, *Good Night, Jackie*, wrote and produced three plays, produced a Saturday morning series with Dad called *Big John, Little John*, (which starred Joyce Bulifant and Robbie Rist), worked as a network executive at ABC on several series (*Happy Days, Laverne and Shirley, Three's Company*, and *What's Happening!*), produced *What's Happening!*, produced the TV movie *Rescue from Gilligan's Island*, wrote and produced a TV movie, *Invisible Woman*, and got married to Barbara—the last event clearly being the most significant.

After the series was cancelled, a phenomenon occurred. The story of the lovely lady and the man named Brady didn't disappear like so many series before and after it. Even while *The Brady Bunch* was running in primetime, ABC needed programming material as it expanded its daytime line-up, and *The Brady Bunch* had just the right amount of wholesome entertainment to fill the bill. The network started syndicating the show, and people were watching in droves.

After we were cancelled, *The Brady Bunch* continued to run in syndication on many cable systems and over-the-air stations. The "little series that could" was more popular, hugely more popular than it had ever been during its original run.

How to take advantage of its new-found cult status? Why not a TV movie that would chronicle what was going on with the characters now? Our own recent TV movie *Rescue from Gilligan's Island* (1978) got a huge rating, so one with the Brady family might do very well, too. It didn't hurt that Dad and I had produced that movie and that the president of NBC, Fred Silverman, had bought that one as well.

So in 1981, *The Brady Girls Get Married* sprang to life.

It was really complicated for us since Dad and I were at Universal doing the series *Harper Valley, P.T.A.* when *The Brady Girls Get Married* was ordered: Two different projects at two different studios.

What made *The Brady Girls Get Married* particularly emotional for me was the reunion theme. When the original series went off the air, there were unaddressed feelings between us and the cast. The split that occurred when some of the kids went with the agent of the devil had never healed itself. Would there still be hard feelings? I didn't know—and wouldn't know until we all would get together on the first day of filming.

The first problem was to see if any of them wanted to do the movie in the first place. That was a relief. Everyone did. Even Robert Reed. For some it was a difficult decision. It is hard for actors who are in series to avoid typecasting, and work wasn't coming easily to the kids who were so identified with the series. Some actors escape it; others don't. But all the *Brady* actors had to come to grips with the fact that they would be going back.

I'll even give Robert Reed credit this one time. When Dad called him, he immediately said "Yes." And that meant getting out of another commitment. Robert said, "There is no way those girls are getting married without their father there."

The story of the TV movie was pretty self-explanatory with the title: *The Brady Girls Get Married.* Marcia and Jan would both get married.

The biggest casting question would be the two husbands. I had two close actor friends, Ron Kuhlman and Jerry Houser, who I used as prototypes when I wrote the movie with Dad. Marcia's husband, Wally, would be an expansive, slap-on-the-back kind of impulsive guy (perfect for Jerry), whereas Jan's husband, Philip, would be a professor and very by-the-book (ideal for Ron). The husbands would each reflect the girls they would marry, except they would be more extreme. We then began looking at actors for the roles of Wally and Philip. We saw 500 actors, and narrowed down to 128 for the second round of casting.

I had the idea of hiring my actress wife, Barbara to read with each of the callbacks while Dad and I and the director would watch and narrow down the casting from there. I've always enjoyed working with Barbara, and we have done many projects together, before and since.

I hadn't thought through my asking Barbara to do this since the two test scenes were romantic proposal scenes. My father and I watched as my wife kissed 128 other men. I know exactly how many because I was counting—and not really liking it. Oh, well, she seemed to enjoy it more than I did.

Eventually, two actors rose above the others and were selected by the network and studio. After our exhaustive search and screen tests, the role of Wally would be played by Jerry Houser and the role of Philip went to Ron Kuhlman, my same two friends who I had been thinking about during the writing. Did I influence the casting because they were friends of mine? Only to bring them in. Maybe I wrote it so much for them that they were the only ones who could play it perfectly. At any rate, they got the parts and were selected by the studio and network all by themselves!

Because of the structure of the story—and the fact that Robert Reed was in a play in New York and only could give us a few days—the cast was assembled as a unit for the first time on the day that we would shoot the wedding.

It was much like a family reunion where people come together for weddings and events. Would there be any awkwardness? No, just the opposite. Each of the kids took a moment to pull me aside and apologize for what had happened at the end of the series. I was very moved. There have been no ill feelings ever since.

Florence came to me and said that she and Robert also had been talking. He told her that he felt bad because he hadn't been very nice to me during the course of the series, and admitted that sometimes he had even gotten upset and downright ornery.

I laughed. "Ornery? Go back and tell him that he skipped 'upset and ornery' and went right to asshole."

She later reported that she told him what I had said and he laughed for 20 minutes.

The spirit on the set for *The Brady Girls Get Married* was wonderful. Everyone got along, and the film itself demonstrated those feelings.

I particularly liked Philip's proposal to Jan, since I used the exact dialogue that I had used in my real-life proposal to Barbara. It was art imitating life.

As for Wally and Marcia, their proposal was more a spur-of-the-moment event that followed a whirlwind courtship.

I decided to play the progress of their relationship in a musical montage. I've never liked those kinds of montages, so I thought I could satirize the montage form by adding humor. It also got me in serious trouble.

Since the series had gone off the air, the six Brady kids had matured into adults. Maureen had become a young woman, and I thought that Jerry and Maureen could have some fun during the montage. Since I knew that there would be music over whatever was said, I gave them permission to say whatever they wanted since we wouldn't be using it anyway. While we were filming them on a boat in the lake, the sound man, Jim Wright, came over to me. Jim was a good Christian, and he was pale. Even though the dialogue would be completely covered by music, Jim had put pinned microphones on Maureen and Jerry anyway, and he was hearing things that he had never heard actors say ever. In fact, I suspected the modest Jim had never heard that kind of language anywhere in his life.

He asked me if I knew what they were saying, and I told him I didn't but that it didn't matter—neither would anybody else since music would be the only sound.

Apparently, Maureen and Jerry took me at my word about saying anything they wanted and said some pretty sexual things. All I know is the network got a lot of letters from lip-readers who were appalled that any Brady show would have such filth. I learned not to do that kind of thing again.

Along with the TV movie, Dad and I had additional plans for a new Brady series. After the girls got married in the story, they and their husbands would move in together and share a house. We thought that it could be a good series about two very dissimilar couples who only live together because the girls are sisters, and it's all they could afford.

On NBC, only one series was winning its time period, our own *Harper Valley, P.T.A.*. Fred Silverman had the idea of cutting up our Brady movie into four parts and scheduling it after *Harper*. He called Paramount and made his proposal. In truth, Fred had been president of ABC when I was an executive, and I knew how his mind worked. I had already been contemplating how I would edit *The Brady Girls Get Married* into four pieces by the time he came up with the idea.

What I hadn't contemplated was Paramount's response. Paramount would only agree to cut up the movie if NBC would order six episodes of a new series, *The Brady Brides*, that would spin out of the movie. Fred Silverman countered. He said that he would order the new series if Paramount made the transition seamless—which meant that there could be no break from the end of *The Brady Girls Get Married* to the beginning of the new *Brady Brides* series. Paramount and NBC happily made their deal and told us about it afterwards. They were thrilled, but we were the ones who had to implement it.

We had been brought into *Harper Valley, P.T.A.* when they were having trouble with the direction of the show. We took it over with no lead time, and we had to hit the ground running with no scripts ahead. We were writing them, or getting them ready with other writers, and barely completing episodes in time to air on a week-to-week basis.

Now, we were asked to do the same thing with *The Brady Brides*. In short, we had two series at two different studios with no advance time at all. I literally found myself going to work at 3:30 in the morning and coming home at 11:30 at night seven days a week for six months. Often times, it was just me and the cleaning crew in my office in the middle of the night.

In the end, it was worth it. *The Brady Girls Get Married* had the highest rating of any TV movie the week it aired. Then we switched from a movie technique to a three-camera comedy technique for *The Brady Brides*—yet one more incarnation of *The Brady Bunch*.

And here come the Brides.

CHAPTER 58

THE BRIDES

When you are in this business, you look for things that are creatively satisfying and things that are monetarily satisfying and are happy to settle for either. In the case of *The Brady Brides*, I was happy with both, and it was nirvana.

I was working with people whom I liked on a project that I liked, and I was only unhappy that it didn't last longer. Our ratings were good enough to be picked up, but Grant Tinker, who was running NBC at the time, didn't appreciate our show and we were cancelled after only six episodes in 1981.

Each of the episodes that we did was fun. We tried some things, had a lot of laughs, and I'm proud of the shows that we did.

It was a new style for *The Brady Bunch*. We were doing the episodes before a live audience in a traditional three-camera technique. Ann B. was in a few episodes, and Florence became a regular on the series and was a natural. Robert wasn't in any episode. Maybe that's why the whole experience was so delightful.

One of the funniest episodes actually came at the suggestion of the network. They concluded that since this show was about brides and grooms, we should see if we could make a deal with *The Newlywed Game* and do an episode where they actually go on the popular game show.

I love fulfilling an assignment like that. Warren Murray, one of our staff writers, went to work immediately, and the two of us turned out an episode script in a week. To this day, I think it remains the funniest episode of any series I ever did.

By this time, John Lenox and I had become full business partners. He was the line producer on *The Brady Girls Get Married*, as well as on *The Brady Brides*. John was adept at making deals and was proud that he made an overall deal that included four main features of *The Newlywed Game*: Bob Eubanks (host), Johnny Olsen (announcer), the set, and the music.

The plot was simple. Bob Eubanks' car broke down near the Brady brides' home, and Bob asked to use the phone. While there, he observed the comedic fighting that went on and offered them the chance to be on *The Newlywed Game*.

They accepted. The result was pandemonium, with all of them sacrificing their dignity.

On the way to the set for the first reading, a thought suddenly came to me: What if Bob Eubanks had never acted before? As far as I knew, nobody asked him that one pertinent question—and hosting a game show is far different than acting. But I dismissed the notion. Certainly, he must have done some acting, even a college class or a high school play. Everyone's done that.

When I was introduced to him, he said, "You know, I never acted before."

In rehearsals, everything went fine. But when the show audience came in and started laughing, he kept talking and didn't pause, so many of his subsequent lines went unheard. We did retakes, and it all ended up fine, but it taught me the lesson to ask the simplest question first.

During one of the rehearsals, Barbara came to the set. We were setting up a scene when everything stopped. I didn't know why. The cast and crew and I had all become good friends, and all of them were in on something that I was unaware of. Barbara gave me a present, and I opened up. It was a picture of a baby. That was how I found out that she was pregnant. Everybody else knew before I did.

What made Barbara's revelation even more ironic was that in *The Brady Girls Get Married*, Greg Brady had become an obstetrician, and Barbara played a woman who was giving birth. She was recently pregnant, so I guess in one way our son, Andrew, was nine months premature.

CHAPTER 59

BROKEN

Between *The Brady Bunch* and *The Brady Brides*, about seven years had passed. Since Dad and I were not involved with *The Brady Bunch Variety Hour* we weren't aware of personal problems that had arisen with the cast, particularly Maureen McCormick. One day during the filming of the first episode of *The Brady Brides*, Maureen didn't show up for rehearsal.

I am very strict about punctuality. I am actually a tyrant on that one point. Maureen's absence threw everything off and was inexcusable, especially since she had offered no excuse, and nobody knew where she was.

I called her agent, Sandy Bressler, who also made no excuse, nor did he tell me of her whereabouts. Instead, Sandy asked me to lunch. I sensed there was something he wasn't telling me.

After we sat down at the table, the first thing he said was, "What are we going to do about our problem?"

"Problem?" What problem?

Sandy went on to say that Maureen had developed a pretty serious cocaine addiction during the years we hadn't been working together, and her failure to report for rehearsal that day was an indication that she was still using.

I couldn't help but feel sorry for Maureen. Being in the public eye is stressful. I only wish I had been more present during the intervening years so that I could have helped her through any difficult times.

I looked at Sandy and asked, "Why didn't you tell me this before?"

"I was hoping it wouldn't be a problem."

"Well, it is."

I told him that he had to tell her to call me.

Maureen didn't call. She showed up to film the next day as if nothing was wrong. I asked her if she was okay. Covering up her misbehavior, she said that she didn't think she was needed for rehearsal the previous day.

We had always been close in the past, and I hoped that my questioning would be enough to keep her clean from that point forward.

I was wrong.

One day when we were filming a scene where the two couples were moving into the house they would share, Maureen didn't show. We called her apartment. No answer. Her agent didn't know where she was. This was serious.

I went to the dialogue coach, Judd Lawrence, and the assistant director and told them to go to her apartment and see if she's there.

They did. They soon called me and said she was inside and had told them through the door that she would be right out.

They waited outside for 10 minutes and knocked again. No answer. They didn't know what do and called me back.

"Break down the door," I said.

They did. They found Maureen collapsed on the bathroom floor.

I didn't know what to do. I had little experience with drug issues, but I did know it was going to be up to me. I told them to drive Maureen to my house.

I left work and went home and talked to Barbara about it before Maureen arrived. I had decided to intervene, but I needed to talk to Barbara first because it would call for a real change of our own life.

"I want to move Maureen into our house."

"For how long?"

"It's important that Maureen knows we care about her. It's not for the length of the show. She can't think that all we care about is the show. And it isn't. I've known her too long. It's got to be open-ended. Maybe forever."

I give Barbara a lot of credit because she didn't take time to blink before she said, "Of course."

Maureen moved into our house. I took her car away from her, and I only allowed her to go to the studio for work and back home with us. I drove her to work myself. She was a veritable prisoner.

Are you permitted to restrict another adult that way? I didn't know. I only knew that I had to do what I could. I called Dad and told him what I was doing.

Maureen was ashamed, but our long history made it so that she trusted me. I think instinctively she knew that I may be her last chance, so she went along with our strict controls.

"Do it," he said.

While she was living with us, I took her to a couple of therapists to see if someone could help her with her addiction. One therapist kept questioning me about my motives—what real interest did I have in Maureen? I explained I had no ulterior motives. I'd known Maureen since she was a girl, and all I wanted to do was help her. I don't think he believed me.

About two weeks after she moved in, I got a call from Maureen's parents who invited me to lunch. Obviously, they had been unable to help their daughter break her drug habit and didn't know where to turn. They appreciated what I was doing.

Her mother said, "We have been praying for an answer, and you're it."

I thought that was odd. Her parents were transferring their own obligation onto me.

On the set, I instructed Judd Lawrence to follow her everywhere and to make sure she was never out of his sight.

Maureen lived with us in "house arrest" for several weeks. Jerry Houser—Maureen's on-air husband—was instrumental in helping us with her. Jerry is quite religious and assisted Maureen in rediscovering her Christian faith.

I'm happy to say that a lot of things came together to change the pattern of Maureen's life.

At one of the meetings at church, Maureen met Michael Cummings. Maureen was smitten, maybe because he wasn't a Brady fan.

By the time she moved out, and was off of drugs, she was into a full-blown relationship with Michael who has been a rock in her life. They've been married for many years.

Parenthetically, there have been some recent revelations of other difficulties that Maureen has faced. She's written a book about her tribulations. In the book, I even found out that she had done some lines of coke when she was in our house. That was something I didn't know. I hope all that is behind her now. I wish her all the best. She's a very sweet person.

CHAPTER 60

A CHRISTMAS PRESENT

When Dad and I aren't doing a project together, I am often off producing or writing other things. When he calls with an idea, we come back together, and it's as if we have been working together straight through. Also, Dad is getting older, and I like to help him as much as I can. It was in 1987 when Dad had an idea for a Christmas movie with the cast of *The Brady Bunch*. As he said, "There is nothing more American than holidays, and no family more American than the Brady family."

I agreed completely. We got together, wrote an outline and went together to Paramount and presented it. Paramount liked the idea and immediately took it to CBS.

At the time, I was working as producer of the series *The Munsters Today*, for which I had written the pilot. If *A Very Brady Christmas* were to sell, I could fit it in and film it during a hiatus.

Then I got a call from Dad, who had gotten a call from Paramount, who had gotten a call from CBS, which wanted to buy the movie.

"That's great!" I said.

"Yeah," he replied.

I could tell from the inflection of his one-word response that there was something he wasn't telling me.

"What is it?" I asked.

"They want the writers of the movie to be me and a woman writer, Gwen Bagni."

It took me awhile to absorb what he was saying before I responded. "You mean they looked at our outline and on the basis of that decided that you are okay to write the movie and I'm not?"

"It looks that way."

"Dad, if that's the way it has to be, okay. I don't want to stand in the way of the movie being done, but I have to tell you that the decision causes me some problems personally."

Dad let me vent.

"I have a career, and the thing that always hangs over it is the belief that *Brady* and *Gilligan* are the only things I can write. Sometimes I beat it, sometimes not, but apparently somebody somewhere is saying I can't even do *Brady*. I want you to do the movie and write it with Gwen Bagni, but I am asking you to please do me one favor. Just find out who has a problem with my writing the movie. I have to find that out and deal with it."

Dad thought I was being reasonable and said he'd get back to me.

After a half hour he called back.

"Well?" I asked.

Dad said, "I didn't ask them."

"You didn't?"

"No. I thought about it. You and I have been doing *The Brady Bunch* a long time together. You wouldn't be around, and it wouldn't be fun. You do so much of the work for me, and it makes things much easier."

"That's what you told them?"

"No. I told them to go fuck themselves."

I could hardly believe it. Sherwood Schwartz, of innocent *Brady Bunch* fame, actually told the network people to "go fuck themselves." Dad explained to them that he always wrote with me. Either they took us both as writers, or there would be no movie. He never asked, and we never found out who the unnamed executive was who thought I shouldn't write the movie.

Dad continued, "That was a half hour ago. Five minutes ago, they called back and said that they would love to have us both write the movie."

The production of *A Very Brady Christmas* was in 1988. That was several years after the last reunion, but it was just as much a reunion this time. The story lent itself to that. Instead of taking a cruise over the holidays, Mike and Carol would pay to have the whole family come back to spend the holidays together.

It meant casting kids for the Brady kids who had gotten married—Greg, Marcia, and Jan. It also meant recasting Cindy for this movie. Susan Olsen (Cindy) in real life was getting married at the time of the filming, so she was replaced as Cindy by Jennifer Runyon. Susan also wanted the same amount of money as Maureen and Eve, who now got more money than the other kids since they had starred in the previous *The Brady Girls Get Married* and *The Brady Brides*. I couldn't blame Susan, but if she got equal money, so would Barry, Chris, and Mike, and the budget couldn't sustain that. Susan chose to have her honeymoon.

One of the most enjoyable tasks for Dad and me was to look at the blueprints of the set and decide how to change the famous Brady house. If Mike and Carol had lived in the same house, and most of the kids had left home, what would they have done to their house? We turned the den into an exercise room, and changed the kitchen by junking the 60s-era avocado and orange décor. We added a window box at the rear window of the kitchen and made it all contemporary.

After the movie aired, a fan sent in a letter and complained that we were too lazy to build the house the way it used to be!

The story had all of the Brady kids return with their families—and problems. Even Alice had problems with Sam, whom she had married in the interlude. In traditional Brady fashion, everything was resolved by the end of the show.

At that point, our idea for the future of *The Brady Bunch* was to do a series of these two-hour movies, usually tied to holidays. If the ratings were good for *A Very Brady Christmas*, we thought America would like to check in with the Brady family every half-year or so.

Our plan was foiled by success. The ratings weren't good—they were spectacular. *A Very Brady Christmas* had the highest ratings of any TV movie over the last two years!

Immediately everyone was talking about a new Brady future. Two more movies were ordered immediately—ironically, on the condition that Dad and I write them. So much for the unnamed executive who thought that a change in writers was needed.

CHAPTER 61

BRADYSOMETHING

CBS, which had aired *A Very Brady Christmas*, was desperate for programming. They asked us if we could change their order for more TV movies and make it a new series instead. We had originally thought that just coming on every six months or so was the best way to keep the franchise fresh, but the network pressed Paramount which opted for a series since that was where the real money was. We were at odds with the studio, and we were forced to revisit the Brady family as a series.

Maureen didn't sign on for *The Bradys*. I guess it was a tradition that there would be Brady girl missing in every new project. Eve didn't do the variety series; Susan didn't do *A Very Brady Christmas* (but did return for this dramatic series); and Maureen didn't do this one. I can't blame them for wanting to get involved in other projects, but their excuse often was that they didn't want to be identified with the series. Sorry. No matter what happens, they always will be.

Since *A Very Brady Christmas* had dramatic underpinnings, we knew that the only way to do *The Bradys* would be to do it as a dramatic show. That would mean a large cast of the husbands and wives and kids. Dad and I asked CBS to schedule the show at 9:00 p.m. since we didn't have little kids at the center of the show. It was the original six Brady kids who had grown up, and they had grown-up problems. Like the groundbreaking series *thirtysomething*, I thought of our new series as "Bradysomething."

Robert was even more cantankerous than usual. He signed the contract and failed to mention that he was teaching Shakespeare at UCLA in the mornings and could only film in the afternoons. We found that out the first day when he didn't show up. It meant completely revising the schedule.

And he was in his factual element in this more dramatic series and questioned everything. In one episode, there was a surprise party for Mike Brady, and Alice came in with a cake with all the candles burning. He complained that no one could light that many candles in that short a time. Ann B. said that she could. He was fuming, and said, "I didn't spend my entire career to end up doing this shit." Ann B. was fed up with Robert after all these years of his negativity, so she said, "Maybe it's time you got a new career." He walked off the set. There was tension most of the time, and maybe it's okay that the series didn't last that long.

There is one area where the network had complete control. That's scheduling. You can talk them into or out of a casting change, a new format, etc., but scheduling is their domain and theirs alone. Maybe that's because they are more concerned about the audience flow from *The Bradys* to the show that would follow. In any event, they refused to discuss the schedule with Dad or me.

CBS didn't take our advice. They scheduled the show at 8:00 p.m. Fridays in our old time spot, our old early hour time spot. Alas, we were facing a very Brady-like *Full House*—filled with little kids—which beat us in the ratings.

The first night we were on I was walking toward my car at the studio with Barry Berg who was my co-producer. It was after filming, and I was going home to watch the show's debut. I am normally a very optimistic person, but this time I was being realistic.

"Barry, there is no reason for America to watch this show. I like it. I think it's a good show, but we're not going to get people to tune in. We're on at the wrong time."

He laughed. He couldn't believe I was serious. What really bothered me was that people would now think that there was no more life in the Brady franchise. Unfortunately, I was right about the low ratings. Our numbers were okay for the first show—which aired as a two-hour episode on February 9, 1990—and actually went up after 9:00 p.m. That spike in ratings kind of proved our point. But in the next few weeks, when we played from 8:00 to 9:00 p.m., the ratings weren't there and the show was cancelled.

Finally, for once and for all, this would surely mean the end of The *Brady Bunch*. . . .

Oops—not so fast.

CHAPTER 62

NOW A MAJOR MOTION PICTURE!

Note to readers: When we started working on *The Brady Bunch Movie*, I began writing day-by-day accounts. This long chapter is culled from all the things that happened during our experience on the movie. Though I didn't really try to have the material published, it did help me keep my sanity during a very trying time.

It was now the mid-90s. *The Brady Bunch* began its original run at the end of the 1960s, and some version had been produced in four separate decades. The Brady family had aired on all of the three major networks, and numerous other stations had rerun it. In the 70s there had even been a *Brady Kids* cartoon show. *The Brady Bunch* had been a one-camera comedy show, a cartoon series, a variety show, two TV movies, and a three-camera comedy show. There had been a stage show in the early 90s, *The Real Live Brady Bunch*, which was a satirical version using the original scripts. It had broken box-office records in several major cities including Chicago, Los Angeles, and New York.

The way we saw it, the only thing missing was a motion picture. And Dad had written a script for one. Its story involved the Brady family seeing a crime and entering the Witness Protection Program. It was written as a straight-ahead Brady movie without any satirical slant. He had shown it to a few people, but no one was interested. Then *The Fugitive*, starring Harrison Ford, hit the theaters. It was a very successful movie based on an early TV series. Brandon Tartikoff, our old friend from TV, was now president of Paramount Pictures. He decided that *The Brady Bunch* should be a motion picture and called Dad, who promptly sent him a copy of his script.

Dad received a rejection for that particular script, but there was still ample enthusiasm for a Brady movie. Why? *Batman*, *The Addams Family*, *Wayne's World*—the TV business was suddenly big movie business.

I thought Dad's script was a bit soft for the new edge in movies, and I felt we had to come up with another way to do the movie that would appeal to the new audience, or the project would die. After some talking, we decided on a story that would have the Brady family being held captive by some escaped convicts. I also believed that it was essential that any new movie should involve some good-natured kidding of the Brady franchise.

We called Brandon and told him that for the movie to work, it had to be a satire. Brandon said that he didn't care. He believed that the Brady name would carry the movie no matter what it was. However, many 60s movies had failed because executives thought the name would carry them. There had to be a reason to make the movie, and for *The Brady Bunch*, satire was the key.

In the new scenario, the convicts would be the voice of the audience and would poke fun at the goody-goody Bradys. I give my father credit for listening to me about this change in tone for the show he created. It took real courage and vision for him to accept this fundamental deviation, but he accepted and agreed with my point of view. He's both incredibly open-minded and practical.

We went to the studio for a meeting. After pleasantries, we got to the matter at hand. The executives from Paramount suggested their own idea for a Brady movie: How Mike and Carol met, their courtship, and the wedding.

This was both a lucky and unlucky proposal. My father is a storyteller, and the suggestion about a genesis movie led Dad to tell the group about the origin of *The Brady Bunch*. I'll skip a lot of it; by now you've read it in his part of this book. But the end of the story is significant. It was something that Dad wasn't particularly interested in doing.

No executive—after hearing Dad's story—would try to convince him to do something he didn't really want to do. That's when I spoke up.

"Dad and I have been talking about another idea."

All eyes were on me. I knew I was about to save the day because I was going to let everybody win. Dad knew he could never get them to do his movie, and we didn't want to do theirs.

"How about the Bradys being held captive in their own home by escaped convicts? It's comedic and adds a life-and-death situation. And as a satire, it would have some real bite to it."

One of the executives quickly described it as "*Desperate Hours* meets *The Brady Bunch* with edge."

Executives love quick comparisons.

Everybody sighed. Then agreement erupted around the room followed by handshakes. Eventually, the script that we wrote was like *Desperate Hours* only in the fact that convicts hold a family captive. The characters are all different, but executives need a previous popular success to justify whatever it is they do.

We got to work writing, and when we turned in our first draft, the executives loved it and had a few suggestions. We loved their notes. Everyone was getting along famously. One real positive recommendation was the addition of another convict—a big menacing sort. We thought in terms of Charles Barkley from the Phoenix Suns. Everyone agreed. They told us that everyone at Paramount, including Brandon, loved the script. He gave it a "green light"—the Holy Grail for filmmakers.

We did another draft and this one, too, was greeted with applause. Nothing would stop the movie now. Besides everything else, I realized that Dad and I were probably the first people ever to satirize their own work.

Think things were rolling? Think again. Not only do seasons change every few months, but so do executives. Bye, bye, Brandon.

Although wildly successful in TV, Brandon really had never been able to fit into or change the movie-making system. That fact—combined with his shoot-from-the-hip style and an unfortunate automobile accident that injured his daughter and required his presence at her bedside—stripped Brandon of the necessarily all-consuming energy needed in the position of President of Paramount.

After changes of command at studios, all hell breaks loose. Whoever comes in as the new president wants to do his or her own projects. Few ventures are spared the axe. Knowing the habitual pattern, we felt doomed.

And matters got worse when we learned that the new studio head would be Sherry Lansing under Stanley Jaffe. Sherry became the new president of Paramount and promptly separated herself from Brandon by condemning all projects based on TV shows. We read this in the trades and understandably felt depressed. However, to her credit, Sherry was smart enough to realize that some of the top-grossing movies for Paramount in the last few years were the *Star Trek* movies, *The Addams Family*, and *Wayne's World*. Clearly something about television was striking a chord in the movie-going audience—as well as stuffing studio coffers.

But at the same time, we heard that Sherry Lansing admitted that she knew little about *The Brady Bunch*. In her mid-forties, she confessed she was too old to have been an original fan and, not having had children, never had the pleasure of looking over small shoulders at the omnipresent *Brady Bunch* reruns. It made sense. Sherry and I were the same age exactly, and when I did the series, none of my friends watched.

Sherry Lansing didn't cancel the project, but instead delegated responsibility for "The Brady Bunch Movie" to younger executives at Paramount.

The first decision that the young execs reporting to Sherry made, was to junk our script. Of course that isn't what they told us, but it's what they did. A red light for our green light. What they explained to us was that Sherry thought that we, the creators of *The Brady Bunch*, were indubitably too close to the series and couldn't give it that satiric spin that was needed. What makes this interesting is that we were also told that Sherry had never read our script and yet was able to come to the conclusion anyway. She didn't even know we had written it with the satiric spin she was asking for.

I asked one of these young executives to get Sherry to read the "coverage"—the report that their own readers wrote about the script. I had seen the coverage—in fact, one of his associates had shown it to me—and knew it said that our script was "brilliant . . . and captured everything a satire should be."

The executive looked at me and, with a straight face, actually said, "There was no coverage." Of course I knew he was lying.

How very CIA of him. Destroy the evidence so no one would have a way to argue with the new president.

How anybody can discern that a script should be thrown out without reading it is a skill that any psychic would be thrilled to possess. To put it succinctly, a lady who never watched *The Brady Bunch* ousted people who made *The Brady Bunch*, all the while candidly admitting she didn't know anything about *The Brady Bunch*.

Then we were told that new writers would be brought in to "tweak" the satire.

How can they just do that? Doesn't Sherwood Schwartz, *Brady Bunch* creator, have any say in this? No. After one sells a show, the buyer purchases the copyright as well. That's what happened on the variety show. Even though Dad is thoroughly identified with *The Brady Bunch*, legally Paramount could do just about whatever it wanted with the franchise.

Enter Laurice Elehwany and Rick Copp. After much searching for writers to attempt this rewrite Laurice Elehwany, famous for one movie, *My Girl*, was chosen as the exact right person to satisfy Sherry Lansing.

In preparation for meeting Laurice, I looked at *My Girl* and couldn't find any comedy in the pleasant little movie. *My Girl* will go down in history as the film that killed off McCauley Culkin with bee stings. Rick Copp was Laurice's new partner. As of this date, I don't remember anything much about him except he had a nervous laugh wherever an opinion should have been. We were grilled about Brady trivia by these two diehard fans. Much of it had to do with Robert Reed, who had recently died among a flock of rumors about his life choices. They assured us that they loved our script. They would never do anything of which we would not thoroughly endorse and approve.

All they were going to do was give the screenplay a little edge.

"A little edge." "Edge" is one of those buzzwords like "top-spin," and both terms inundate most meetings by people who seem to know the lingo and not much else. Since they loved our script, obviously there was no need to worry.

There was nothing for us to do but wait for our baby to come back from its first overnight stay.

Dad was out of town when I got a call. Laurice and Rick had a unique idea. How about bringing the 70s Bradys—exactly as is—into the 90s? It was revolutionary, and it would help them write with a more satirical "edge."

Bring the Bradys into the 90s? How?

Well, why not leave them just as they are—with their 70s look and their 70s mentality?

I liked the idea immediately. Besides, I've never argued with passionate writers without letting them try whatever they believe in. Besides, if for some reason this concept didn't pan out, we always had our script to fall back on. I called Dad who liked this new angle, too, and both of us agreed to let Rick and Laurice have a shot at the approach. They were told to go ahead.

A few weeks later, the script arrived.

I've worked on many shows and on many scripts. I'm never really satisfied with any draft—even my own. Dad is even more of a perfectionist than I am. However, we have never sent a script off to rewrite and then had it come back without a single word of our original draft in it. And sadly, what replaced it was thoroughly off-putting. They simply destroyed the characters.

Whatever you or I think of *The Brady Bunch*, you must admit that it is a show that is revered by millions of people. The characters are indelibly imprinted on the American psyche. Laurice and Rick's satirical style was a slashing one.

Apparently, they believed that everyone dislikes the Bradys and wants to put them down. Therefore, their idea of satire and the dreaded "edge" is to trash the show mercilessly—not a good way to endear yourselves to those who created it.

I'm not a prude, but it was pretty distressing to read pages about high school boys all wanting to "get into Marcia's pants" and "pop her cherry." Or scenes where Mike Brady has become hopelessly inept as an architect and takes a job as a fry cook at a hamburger stand. The Bradys move to Hollywood Boulevard and live among street gangs and hookers. Alice is sex-mad and jumps all door-to-door salesmen. Jan is a total psychotic. Bobby and Cindy visit a sperm bank. Packs of stereotypical screen lesbians are on the prowl for Marcia. At every turn the script is filled with profanity and lewd behavior. Needless to say, we didn't exactly do cartwheels over their "edge."

The film that they wrote would have been lucky to get an "R" rating. We didn't give notes; we couldn't. At first, we stated that notes were not relevant. It was a sow's ear. That's all that can be said.

Dad and I kept repeating that an affectionate satire was the only way to proceed. We would never get a wide audience with a movie that merely took an axe to *The Brady Bunch.*

In every one of our meetings we had been assured that Paramount would never march ahead with any project that Dad and I didn't bless. It would be like trampling over Gene Roddenberry on the way to *Star Trek I*, *II*, etc. They thought the Brady franchise had the same kind of future and needed us to make sure it was true to the original.

We couldn't just sit by. We finally wrote blistering pages of notes detailing exactly how their script had to change if we were to find it acceptable. The writers did two or three more drafts and never changed the tone of the movie.

We finally had to play the only card we had to play. Sherwood Schwartz is a brand name. It wouldn't do for Paramount to have him (and me) turn against the movie. By this time, Dad had hired my younger brother Ross as his legal representative.

We instructed Ross to write Paramount a letter that acknowledged Paramount controlled the franchise and could green light any movie they wanted, but Paramount would have to acknowledge that his clients were individuals, and as individuals could go on any talk show and advise the world not to see the movie, which his clients were prepared to do immediately.

Paramount responded. Apparently, they were afraid of us keeping our word. A memo came out which had all of our notes about the script. And this memo went to the writers for a rewrite. The only change from our memo was the letterhead—our names were removed and a Paramount executive's name was inserted, as if our notes were his notes.

Alan Ladd, Jr. was brought in to produce the movie, and Betty Thomas was hired to direct. Bonnie and Terry Turner were the new writers, and we were told they were big fans and knew all the episodes.

That same evening a writer friend of mine called and said he got a call from the Turners who wanted him to tell them about *The Brady Bunch* since they told him they had never seen it.

Before the movie was taken over by Paramount and Alan Ladd, Jr., we had met actress Christine Taylor and thought she'd be perfect for Marcia and told Paramount's casting executives about her. All we ever wanted to do was contribute. We didn't have to run the movie; we just wanted to make it better. Why was everyone threatened by us? I guess power-mad people think that all people are power-mad.

We finally were invited to a casting meeting. It grew serious when they told us that the budget would only allow look-alikes or good non-stars for the other roles. They were talking about Barry Bostwick for Mike Brady. I like Barry and think he's a good actor, but how can you compare him to the names who are added to movies to make them events? Like Jack Nicholson in *Batman*, Harrison Ford in *The Fugitive*, or John Goodman in *The Flintstones*? By going with merely capable actors, they were forcing *The Brady Bunch* itself to be the only draw. That and the fact that it's a satire.

Nobody has more fondness for *The Brady Bunch* than I do, but I didn't see why people would go to the movies and pay when they could get *The Brady Bunch* for free every day. I suggested Madonna or Mia Farrow for Carol Brady. They blanched and told me the obvious: Madonna and Mia were expensive and carried a lot of baggage. I told them it was "good baggage"—what they would bring to the movie would be the unexpected. Let Madonna say pristine Carol Brady lines, and it's funny. With Mia Farrow's image due to her situation with Woody Allen and all those kids, she would bring a quirkiness to the role, as well as being a fine actress.

As a last stab at interesting casting I suggested Barbara Mandrell for Carol and Christopher Reeve for Mike. Barbara has a country music background which mimics Florence Henderson's Indiana roots. And Superman for Mike? That ethos makes it both ironic and interesting.

Alan Ladd, Jr. said, "Barbara Mandrell is too tall."

What? "Too tall?" To myself, I imaged Barbara Mandrell and concluded that she is about five feet tall. Besides, what did her height have to do with anything?

Ladd explained. "Everybody knows that a lot of the humor in *The Brady Bunch* is that Mike is so tall and Carol is so short."

Oh, really? First of all, I'd been doing the Brady saga for a quarter of a century, and this was the first I'd heard of size differential being a big subject of humor—or *any* subject of humor. Florence Henderson is five foot three and Bob Reed was six foot two. There was never a single reference to their disparate heights in any episode.

At the end of the day they hired Gary Cole for Mike and Shelley Long for Carol. Shelley is five foot eight, and in heels is as tall as Gary Cole.

The day-to-day producing was done by an attractive capable blonde producer named Jeno Topping, a name which always sounded to me like something you put on Jello.

My first trip to the studio engendered every conceivable human emotion. Try to put yourself in my place as I walked into Stage Five, the same stage where we filmed all five years of the series and where I spent every waking moment during that time.

Now, I walked in and the set was exactly the same, having risen like the Phoenix. And all the Bradys who were on it looked very much like the people I had known decades ago, but they weren't them. It was surreal, like the dream many of us have as children in which we get home and there are other people living in our house and don't recognize us.

The children playing Bobby and Cindy, Jesse Lee Soffer and Olivia Hack, were playing on the swing-set just as the original Bobby and Cindy had for so many years. I crossed to them.

We talked a bit, and I told the kids about the "bush fish" that lived in the plastic bushes on the set.

Their eyes widened as they said they haven't seen them.

The new Bobby and Cindy were just as gullible as Mike Lookinland and Susan Olsen had been, and started asking questions. Children are children. I made a note to tell Mike and Susan that the bush fish were alive and well. Mike Lookinland, now with children older than the new Bobby was, definitely would appreciate it.

After seeing some of the shooting and after reading the latest script, I was beginning to think that the movie would be successful in spite of everything.

After the film was edited and went through post-production, I picked up Dad for the drive to Paramount to go to a screening of the movie. We arrived at the studio and went to the theatre where a lot of exec types were waiting outside while the 400-person research audience waited inside. There was nervous chatter among the concerned.

The movie went extremely well. The executives were bubbling over and practically giddy.

The audience appreciated each and every reference to Brady episodes.

And this was not a stacked sampling. These people had been selected as a cross-section of moviegoers. The group of Paramount researchers carefully noted the specific moments of laughter and boredom to chart how the film will be changed.

Dad and I turned to Betty Thomas who had recorded every reaction. Even though the screening was a success, there were some problems, and we all knew what they were. Every note we had given them, which they had ignored, now was a problem.

Fortunately, everyone (audience and executives alike) agreed. The movie soared when it poked good-natured fun at the Bradys and dropped when it strayed.

The comments were precisely what we thought they'd be. The audience loved every time Mike Brady started one of his overstated lectures—a device that Dad and I created in our draft. They loved Jan's satirical over-the-top obsession with Marcia—another device that Dad and I created. They loved the perfect casting of Christine Taylor as Marcia—an actress we selected. They loved using references to Brady episodes—a style we initiated. They loved the over-the-top exaggerated nature of the film—a device of ours.

Okay, I'm blowing my own horn, but are you getting the point? Everything they loved about the film was what Dad and I proposed.

Like a football team around a coach, at the rear of the theatre everyone surrounded Sherry Lansing for words of wisdom and the next play.

Sherry was enthusiastic.

"It's going to be huge."

Sherry then turned to Dad and me.

"And we have to thank Sherwood and Lloyd for this."

Then Sherry pulled me aside and said with great sincerity, "I never told you this before, but *The Brady Bunch* was my favorite show when I was a little girl."

I smiled and walked away. Amazing. Sherry Lansing and I are exactly the same age, and I was producing the series when she was a little girl. It made me realize once again that alternate reality is a place where executives are very comfortable living.

The movie was a major hit: Very good reviews and a great box office.

A friend of mine told me that he talked to executives about the movie and how it all came about. He heard the company line:

"The Schwartzes wrote a long *Brady Bunch* episode and, thank God, we decided that it should be a satire."

CHAPTER 63

AND THEN THE SEQUEL

Of course, there was going to be a sequel. If a studio wants a sequel, there will always be a sequel.

The studio decided it would be about Carol's first husband returning and what problems that would cause.

We didn't like it for several reasons. First, it was about the parents. Second, it was a thin idea with not enough story. Third, all the beats were the same as the first movie. Paramount paid no attention to our objections, but neither Dad nor I were willing to fight them again. It had been too emotionally draining the first time around.

Paramount was proud and happy that they landed Tim Matheson for the role of the former husband. I like Tim. He's a good actor, but at least they should have a major star fighting over Carol. How about Ted Danson? There would be that Sam/Diane thing from *Cheers*. Or Burt Reynolds? Somebody who is formidable. Paramount assured me that Tim was coming out in a big movie, and that he'd be perfect. A Paramount assurance? I knew how much that meant.

Eventually, I came to believe that none of it mattered. They were going to do what they wanted to do. I have learned one rule about the studio system: It's much more important to them that they make *their* movie than a *good* movie.

The sequel was doomed. My last words to them before they went off to make

A Very Brady Sequel were: Don't tell that story; don't call it that; and don't put those people in it.

They didn't listen. I read one draft of the movie and didn't like it much. I went to the set a couple of times. I went to an early screening of the picture and didn't like it much.

Audiences didn't come.

I still have never seen the final version of the movie.

CHAPTER 64

WASHINGTON IN CANADA

We made *The Brady Bunch in the White House* for television in 2002, just as the Fox Network was deciding that they didn't want to make any more TV movies. That meant no money for advertising, which resulted in nobody knowing it was on.

Oh, well, I really like the movie. I wrote it with my sister, Hope, and it is just what I think a *Brady Bunch* satirical movie should be. I was the executive producer as well. It uses *The Brady Bunch* to poke fun at something else—politics and Washington. We also had other ideas for a series of movies: *The Brady Bunch in Amityville*, *The Brady Bunch in Space*, and *A Very Brady Shipwreck*. As with *The Brady Bunch Movie* and *A Very Brady Sequel*, *The Brady Bunch in the White House* stars Gary Cole and Shelley Long as Mike and Carol again, and we recast new kids.

I like Gary and Shelley. Before we started working together, I went to lunch with both of them separately. I didn't go into any of my frustrations with the first movies, but I needed to let them know who I was and that I was now running this movie. They both understood, and we all got along famously.

Gary is one of the easiest actors to work with. Shelley is more demanding, but not in a Robert Reed kind of way. They each cared a lot about what they were doing, and I'd work with both of them again in a minute.

Things come full circle. When we did *A Very Brady Christmas*, a young executive at Paramount, Marcy Pool, was our point person for the studio. Now she was running Fox TV movies. It's too bad that her department was cut loose the week before filming so she never got to promote the movie the way it should have been. It came and went before anyone knew it was on.

The story: Through a series of odd twists of fate, Mike becomes President of the United States and promptly names Carol Vice President. The whole family moves into the White House and manages to turn the entire political establishment upside down.

We filmed it in Toronto. Neal Israel directed and did a great job. We had fun mimicking the style of *West Wing*, and Hope and I even had the audacity to write lyrics to "Hail to the Chief." We used computer technology to have Presidents George W. Bush and Bill Clinton in attendance at the Brady Inauguration.

When we were casting in Toronto, an actor came in to read for Neal and me for the part of one of the FBI men. At the end of the casting session, he asked for our names. I told him, "Lloyd Schwartz." He fainted. He actually fainted.

When he revived, he told us that he was a huge fan of the show and that he had seen my name for years on the screen and never thought he'd actually meet me.

I guess stars get that reaction, but it was pretty unusual for me.

One other interesting thing happened during casting. We were looking for a beautiful girl to play Marcia's rival, Kim Semler. In the dream sequence, Marcia fantasizes that Kim is being taken away to be executed in the electric chair. (Remember, this was a satire.) We asked each of the beautiful girls to scream and yell and plead for her life as they are being dragged away. Each of the girls yelled, but only a controlled yell, even though Neal and I begged them to be more emotional. Afterwards, we thought about it and realized that truly beautiful women don't have experience begging for anything. We eventually had to cast a *pretty* girl instead of a *beautiful* girl, and the scene went fine.

From *The Brady Bunch Variety Hour* to *A Very Brady Sequel*, Dad and I were given the credit or blame for a lot of things we had very little to do with. For *The Brady Bunch in the White House*, I am very happy to take credit or blame since it was the movie that I wanted to do. If you get a chance, rent the DVD and tell me what you think.

CHAPTER 65

ANOTHER REUNION

Besides our Brady projects, there have been others that weren't ours. Some have been authorized, like Susan Olsen's *Brady Bunch Home Movies* (1995) and Barry Williams' TV movie *Growing Up Brady* (2000). There have been documentary specials and an episode of *E's True Hollywood Stories*. In fact, *E! True Hollywood Story: The Brady Bunch* (1999) was the first THS installment to be two-hours long and is the highest-rated episode that series has ever had. There was also our own *Bradymania: A Very Brady Special* (1993). The cast has been on game shows and reality shows and depicted themselves on other series, and no show has had so many reincarnations.

One unwelcome Brady show was a Fox TV unauthorized special that aired in 2002. It was a totally untrue fabrication of events that simply never took place. It's amazing what free speech allows. The less said about it the better. I'll just say their "Lloyd Schwartz" was presented as a chain smoking little weasel who swore at everyone and had no talent. I have never smoked; I'm not short; and I don't swear. As for no talent; that's subjective.

Fortunately, the experience came and went and I soon had another chance to work on a successful *Brady Bunch* project.

At the TV Land Awards in 2004—ironically honoring *Gilligan's Island* with a Pop Culture Award—I ran into Sal Maniaci who is head of programming for the TV Land network. *The Brady Bunch* has been a staple of their line-up, and Sal and I got to talking about doing a show. That talk would soon evolve into the 35th anniversary of *The Brady Bunch.*

We quickly put together the anniversary show and titled it: *Still Brady After All These Years*. Hope and I would write it and produce it with Sal and Michael Petok. It aired on TV Land later in 2004 and was hosted by Jenny McCarthy. After a lot of negotiating we managed to get all of the Brady kids and Ann B. Davis and Florence to appear at the same time.

There were a lot of laughs and some tears, but the highlight was having them all reminisce about their experiences together. These moments were interlaced with clips. It ended with them all going up on the stairs and assuming the same positions they have taken so many times before. The studio audience gave that moment a standing ovation.

When the ratings came in, it was a big hit for TV Land and received some of their biggest numbers ever. It was rerun many times. It also received a Daytime Emmy Nomination. We knew we wouldn't win; we were in the specials category and the well-deserved Emmy went to a salute to the 911 victims.

Just in case, however, I wrote an acceptance speech that was never delivered:

"As long as *The Brady Bunch* was on the air in prime time, we never won an award, and now this. I think we should have skipped the series completely and have gone right to this reunion special."

CHAPTER 66

MUSICALLY SPEAKING

At the TV Land Awards in 2008, *The Brady Bunch* won the Pop Culture Award. Everybody showed up, except for Eve. No surprise there. I just wish her happiness and an understanding that she will forever be Jan Brady and loved by millions.

It was a great year of recognition for Dad. He was awarded a star on Hollywood Boulevard at the age of 92 and, at the ceremony—since *No Country for Old Men* had just won the Best Picture Oscar—he sharply commented, "This isn't just a country for old men."

In November 2008 Dad entered the Television Academy Hall of Fame, an honor given to just over a hundred men and women. He is finally getting his due.

And I continue to do what I do. I've got several TV projects in the works, lots of theatre, and it looks like Warner Brothers is finally going to do a big *Gilligan's Island* feature film with Dad and me as executive producers. While *Gilligan's Island: The Musical* has had many successful productions all around the country and has just concluded a national tour, one request has kept coming from the various theaters it has played: Can they do the *Brady Bunch* musical next? We have always turned them down for one basic reason: There wasn't a "*Brady Bunch* musical."

Hope and I decided to end that problem by writing *A Very Brady Musical* in 2008. Hope married Laurence Juber, an accomplished guitarist and composer who had played in Wings with Paul McCartney. All of us—except for Paul McCartney—did *Gilligan's Island: The Musical* together, and Laurence has been the composer on several Gilligan and Brady projects. Since the time that Dad, I, Laurence and Hope wrote the Gilligan musical, I've had a lot of experience in doing musicals. Two that I have written—*Jubilee* and *You & Me*—have had local productions in Los Angeles and have won awards.

In addition, I have written and/or co-written and/or directed 18 children's musicals that have had productions at Theatre West in Los Angeles. Hope and Laurence have written four of those with me as well. Theatre West is where Barbara and I founded Storybook Theatre of Los Angeles, where it has been in residence for the last 25 years and is the only Equity children's theatre in Los Angeles. Those musicals have been very successful, have won dozens of awards and commendations, and have resulted in our being honored by the U.S. Senate and House of Representatives. I've even won the Red Carpet Award from Women in Theatre, though I'm not sure if that now makes me a woman in theater or not.

Do I sound proud of everything that our children's theatre has accomplished? Absolutely. I'm prouder of what we've done with Storybook Theatre than of anything with which I have ever been involved. So even though I have never thought of myself as being a particularly musical person, I have somehow accumulated a body of work that makes some people feel otherwise, sometimes even me.

At any rate, Hope and I got to work on the plot of the musical. We wanted *A Very Brady Musical* to have the satirical tone of the feature movies with all original songs by Hope and Laurence.

The story is all based on a misunderstanding. The kids overhear the parents having a violent argument and think that Mike and Carol are heading for a divorce. Of course, what they actually had heard was their parents reading a play called *I Hate Your Guts* that was written for a P.T.A. fundraiser. Each of the kids decides to raise money in a unique fashion. Greg will run a taxi service; Marcia sees an ad for an escort service and mistakenly believes that "dating for money" is just that; Peter and Jan will put on magic shows on street corners; and Bobby and Cindy will look for money that people accidentally lose. Of course by the end of the play, Greg is arrested for bank robbery as his car is used as a getaway car; Marcia is taken downtown for prostitution; Peter and Jan, who accidentally use the wrong saw and almost cut a man in half, are jailed for attempted murder; and Bobby and Cindy end up behind bars for picking pockets.

Another aspect of *A Very Brady Musical* that intrigued me was its Brady way of saluting Broadway musicals. Each of the songs is from a different musical-comedy genre so we poke fun at *The Sound of Music*, *Grease*, *Annie*, *Sweet Charity*, and others. This was the only bone of contention between Hope and me. She didn't like being placed in the box of writing songs like other songs, but we agreed to disagree, and it somehow ended up satisfying both of us.

Theatre West is a company of actors, and I had worked with many young people who had been in the Storybook Theatre plays. In thinking about who would be what character, I realized that we had everybody we needed within the company without having to cast outside.

Now the time came to pick a director. I needed someone who knew the material, knew the theatre, knew the actors and could deliver the play in a short amount of time. I decided on . . . me. Rather than spending a lot of time explaining what I wanted to someone else, I figured it would just be easier for me to do it.

A date was set, and we started work on the sets, costumes, and rehearsal. It's not to say that it went off without a hitch. We lost actors along the way, and redid the set and the music, but the end result was a play that—I am proud and relieved to say—received wonderful reviews and packed houses.

One interesting change was to the role of Greg. It had to do with my son Elliot. Elliot is eight years younger than my son Andrew, and whereas Andrew has become a writer, Elliot has always been a performer. When we began casting *A Very Brady Musical*, I cast Elliot as Peter. Elliot has been in lots of our Storybook Theatre plays, has won "Best Actor in a Children's Play," and had the lead in most of his high school plays. In addition, he is now in the theatre department at UCLA.

During rehearsal, the actor playing Greg had a schedule conflict when another play he was doing got extended. Unable to do both, he respectfully bowed out of *A Very Brady Musical.* What to do? I looked around and saw Elliot. The part of Greg had a lot more to do than the role of Peter, but I knew that Elliot would be up to the task. He switched and became the oldest brother. It was ironic since in real life, Elliot is much younger than all the rest of the actors playing the other kids, but he is taller, and on stage he really made it work. Due to his performance, an agent signed him, he was offered a role in a TV pilot and he was brought in to audition for the national tour of a different musical.

There have been lots of offers for *A Very Brady Musical* to move to other theaters. Even a Broadway presentation is in the works.

In addition, I've even written a film script of the musical since musicals starring young people are now in demand.

It all just keeps going on, and on, and on—doesn't it?

Indeed, *The Brady Bunch* has left the land of television and has entered Americana. References continue to be made, and probably always will be.

Other than a path for *A Very Brady Musical*, are there more Brady projects in the works? Absolutely. The latest is this book.

Another possibility is a reality series which would find a new blended family and move them into an exact replica of the Brady house.

Yet another new series idea is one which Dad and I created and will be as unique as the original series was. It's a black/white series where a white man with three daughters marries an African-American woman with three sons. We are also discussing the possibility of making it Latino/Anglo which would celebrate the differences between the cultures. In this era of Barak Obama, blending two families of different races is an idea that deserves to be on television. Even Michelle Obama has publicly declared that she can identify every episode of *The Brady Bunch*.

The Brady Bunch just keeps rolling along. In 2010, *TV Guide* had a rating of the 50 greatest TV families. And the Brady family beat out everyone from the Huxtables to the Simpsons and was number one.

Will it ever end? Only when the people don't want more.